New Journal Writers

Writers

Volume Three

Hills of Light

2013

Ronald Collins, editor

1st Edition – 2013

ISBN-13: 978-1483931425
ISBN-10: 1483931420

cover photo by
GC Photography and Video

Contents

Dedication

We would like to dedicate this volume to Memories of
Darius Czarnota
and
Deborah Nash

taken too young and dearly missed.

Preface

This is the third volume of the Newfound writers series. The first volume, *Shadows of Water*, was focused on the work of local poets, and the second volume, *Angles of Life*, expanded the range to include prose and art. This volume includes short stories and even an historical piece.

We also have in this collection our first "spooky" stories centered around local myth. Several of the writers in this collection were mesmerized by the light and beauty and serenity found at Newfound Lake.

The works are in alphabetical order by the writer's name.

The title *Hills of Light* was chosen to reflect the beauty of Newfound evenings and early morns when the light can stun you into silence.

Collins Publishing

Gary Altheim

A New Found Me!

Newfound Lake, a new found Me
My poem, my life, here you will See

A Miracle my book started on Newfound Lake
Finally, as many requested for goodness Sake

A Newfound Lake poem, a re-found me, please take a Look
A psychologist, photographer, poet and writer of Books

Growing up on Newfound Lake, since going to Camp
I yearn to earn the Newfound poetry Stamp

Many life lessons I have learned Here
Tools I take with me when I am not Near

Smart people learn from their own Mistakes
Wise people from others their wisdom Take

The wise don't need to make errors to See
They can learn from others, please take it from Me

As a child at age Eight
I came to Newfound Lake

My parents wanted to get rid of Me
For 2 months every summer you See

As the Captain of the Blue Buccaneers Team
To the campers I was "the man" so it Seemed

The need to replenish brought me back to Newfound
I was a carrying a weight, like that of a trillion Pound

So I said to myself I need to go back to that beautiful Place
Bring back my Chi and put a smile on my Face

What I miss very much is Theo and Nehri
Without them sometimes it's hard to be Merry

This Newfound beauty is a place of Peace
On a quiet clear night all my troubles Cease

The sky and stars are spectacular, Unreal
Pause and look up, the source you can Feel

Newfound Lake, please help me give up my Will
Breathe, fresh air, relax, write, and sit Still

If I do that my bucket with energy I Fill
Chi, power from the earth, no need for a Pill

Overwhelmed by emotions as I settle at Coppertoppe
Rushing thoughts and feelings, my pen can't Stop

Yesterday sunny, cold and Nice
Today, snow and fog cover the Ice

The lake is gorgeous either Way
Frozen or clear blue is what I Say

Emotions, I am very sensitive, I need a Gate
Injustices, politics, fraud, and narcissism I Hate

Atop Newfound Lake I was taught many a Thing

Inhale, Exhale, flow, Chi, spirituality and soon I am sure we will Sing

The car in front of me said Miracle on the Plate
A vacation for me after 7 years, follow the Bait

Anything is possible even a vacation
The warrior in me needs salvation

Work, family, my life was Insanity
At Newfound now comes Serenity

Newfound lake, still light enough I can just See
The Clouds, the plants, the mist, thru the Trees

Loving nature, Newfound Lake, it's part of the Key
Learning, it's all about you, and it's all about me

Like First Nation cultures, today I did Learn
I am what I am, please be nice, don't Discern

Camp Tomahawk inspired my Camp called Excel
Started when witnessing youth going through Hell

Inner-city kids never at a lake so they Tell
The sight of the wildlife we did not Sell

For the campers and families it's Free
Just to get out of the city, nature to See

Sing the Camp Cheer
Have no Fear

It's safe to shed a Tear
Ohave means love, that's our dog, he is Here

He lies there on the living room Floor
Protecting his Gary and the Inn's front Door

Learned all life has emotions, on this new-found-me Shore
The strength of the lake keeps my heart and soul to the Fore

Clouds of gray cover Newfound Lake's Sky
For me a great place to play, cry, and live Free or Die

Nature's spirit and beauty give you a natural High
Leaving is hard, be grateful, pull away, give a Sigh

In New Found Me, never-ending soul lessons Lie
On Newfound Lake, say Farewell, not Goodbye

Jan Collins

Advice

We listen with much thought
Yet question the advice given
What does it mean? To us? To others?
Listen, think and then move forward
So much to learn,
Find the balance and live, love and learn.

Birches

Birches are bare
White and bright
They bend and sway
With the spring winds
Then leaves come with bright of green
They sway all summer, then golden with fall
So graceful and limber
So serene and peaceful
Birches are a symbol
and feed our need for nature

Hills

Rolling hills, the start of the great
Dips and valleys
Points and peaks
Lead to the Great Whites
Tall and great
The hills hold so many secrets and stories
Of times gone by
History abides in these hills for all of us to explore

Spring

The glow of the buds
Purples violets and browns
The start of a new year for our special hills
They reflect in these waters, glow in the sunsets
They grow into buds
Some into leaves and some into flowers
Spring brings us freshness and an awakening of the hills.

New buds, warm sun, and new sunsets
These give us the feel of a new spring
Birds singing and the loons coming back to the lake
All the ducks gather to great us at the beach
This starts a new beginning with each year a fresh start
Buds, bees buzzing
Dining on the deck
all start a new spring on Newfound

The Glow of Life

A splash of a fish
The merganser fluttering
The call of a loon
These are the sights and sounds of the new beginning
A new year ahead
A summer of fun
Wildlife, real life, kids, family and friends
It is all a happening of life on Newfound
And the joy of living is a glow of life

Ice Out - 2012

It usually comes late in April but this year it was March
Early and strange but so nice to see
We love the lake, the ice, and then the ice out
Spring leads to summer and after the heat
comes our favorite time of fall.
September is the best for hiking and relaxing and
THEN it's time for ice again.

The Past

We will never be what we were
Yet we have become so much more
Changes in life brings changes in us

Education

To know is to believe
To Believe is to question
To question is to learn
To learn is to know

Family

Love is unconditional
Worry is normal
for we always want to protect
Our loved ones
Yet, decisions determine our life
We will love forever
but not always like
The ones that mean the most to us
We need to accept ourselves and others
Even if we do not agree or like the differences
Love draws us together
and overpowers our differences

Questions

Who am I and What will my life mean?
The unknown always brings me with one more question
How do we learn by asking questions?
Life is not clear and we need experience, time and care to
Try and find our answers.
Are there answers?
Sometimes, but not always
Life throws us so many curves
Yet, we need to try to find answers.

Light

Light on the mountains
Light on the hills
Brings a feeling of hope and peace
Light makes us feel good
Yet too much makes us feel bad
Balance is the secret
we need light to survive and feel alive

So Different

We all are important and our thoughts are real
Yet we all come from different worlds of thought
Some are the here and now and
some are the much bigger view.
They are all important and one without the other does not exist
We need people to work with all thoughts and ways of thinking
To make our world whole and one.

Today

If there is never another today
That is OK
Today was perfect
Good weather, good temp,
Good feelings, good fun and good life
That's what makes it OK
Peace with the world
But more important is peace with
Life and ourselves

Flashing

Lights, life, years and more
Where does all the flashing go or come
Life flashes before us everyday
Before we know it, it is gone
Catch the flashes and grab the time to enjoy
Every moment and every flash

To Deb

You are so vibrant
A dancer in the stars
Why does life take you?
No one knows but always
Know how special your life has been
To all the people you have touched
And all the joy you have given
Just you and life and what you have given to all

Fall

We are here loving it all
Color, life, leisure
Does it get any better?
Not for me
Life has been good
Kids are my treasures and my life
Home, husband, friends and life in general
are the best I could ask for
Thanks

Ronald W. Collins

Hills of Light

We are little specks of life
in endless eons of time.

And morning came
as light upon the hills
and we are alive.

Death is a natural part
of the journey through life,
and at its time
our little speck
will be as light
upon the hills,
brilliant, fading,
then gone.

Sprinkles of Life

Brilliant specks in a dark place
like stars near at hand.
And life lives us so.
We flash and are gone.
No more anything after we are gone,
just like it was before we were.

D.

It was a sunny day
and near at hand
was a boat you had
swum to a million times.
What did you see
standing on that dock
ready to dive and swim?
The boat was so near
as you clove the water.
Above the water the sun shone,
the birds swooped and sang,
and below you were gripped
by a force you did not
know existed until it
grabbed you and held on,
until, strong as you were,
you could not break free
and all that was happening
above the water meant nothing,
the whole world was you
and your struggle to breath,
and then the world ended.

Observers of Life

We are all observers
and participants in life.
Unasked for, we came to be,
and unwillingly we will go,
but along the way
we watch, and wallow in life,
we spread life all over us,
and watch to see
what life will bring next.

On Sunset Lake

The lake is called Newfound
but tonight the light
at sunset said otherwise,
said now, said really now,
said never again this sunset.
We've seen hundreds, thousands of sunsets,
and yet each one is different,
is enough to make you stop
and look and say wow,
say now, tonight, just the two of us
can see this special light
new found each evening on Sunset Lake.

Beginnings and Ends

It seems that mornings and evenings
are when we are most in the world.
The early light promises a new day,
with promises of something better
than yesterday proved to be.
Rarely does it work out that way
but hope really is eternal.
By the evening sunset we know
what has passed, and what promises were kept:
not many and of those, most only in part.
Yet each day we wake looking forward
each day to all of the possibilities and
disappointments.

Eyes of Yesterday

I look out today through my father's eyes.
I can almost feel him seeing the world
through me.

When I open my eyes to watch a scene,
he probably saw a thousand times,
he is there inside me looking out.

And I welcome him there…

And hope I will be there to see
the world through my son's eyes
when I too am but a memory.

Four Haikus

Learn more to fear less
knowledge sets you free to be
open to embrace more

re-examine all
everything you think you know
always more to learn

"faith" is ignorance
says "I do not know" and "I
do not want to know"

It's not what we know
that we fear - from not knowing
comes pain - learn less fear

The Phoenix

She is an enigma wrapped in a shell
but for those little ones she loves so dear
she is willing to break that shell
and bend her mind, and body,
to do whatever needs to be done
so they are not seared
by the flames that consumed her,
and persevere she will
until her time comes
and she rises once again

Willie P.

It was always "Bill"
though sometimes
when annoyed "William"
but usually just "Bill"

"Will you still love me
when I'm sixty-four?"
and now you know,
though how strange that
now you are "Willie".
Where did that come from?

The decades have shaped us
and more erosion
is yet to come with time
but still there is a core
of solid you and me.

Real World Comfort

The world ends when we do.
There will not be any more
after we leave
than there was
before we were.
How short,
the history of the world,
it starts when we do
and ends when we end.
Except the real world
will go on
as if we never were.

The World Not Us

There is a world
that is not us.
Our world of family,
everyday wants and desires
is a limited world
and some live only there
even though
another world of stars,
atoms and universes
is so there.
The whole world
is both that limited
by who we are
and that that was
and will be forever more
not us but
eternal nevertheless.

Endless Sunsets on Hills of Light

The sun set in a haze
of purple and lavender
behind the hills
layer upon layer
the light faded
as range after range
the hills grew dark
after having
brighten up our evening
as one more day
slipped away
as countless have
and we look forward
to the few
that are left us

Memories of Forest

Deep in woods
smelling of pine and
wet moss
the forest pressed
around me
as it has
countless times before
where dark under trees
provides the coolness
of sylvan shade
to me and my
heated thoughts
and when I leave
the forest will shade
others in need
of the dark

For Deb

the end must come
for all of us
for you earlier
than it should
but in the end
does it matter
it is always now
there is only now
so whenever
our time comes
it will be now
and the world
will carry on

Flash

the world is endless
before we were
and after we are gone
so our little time here
is more a flash
than a duration
but it is our flash
and we should
light up our time
with all we have
to sparkle and dazzle
in our short time
under the sun

Green Forest, Pure Sound

Crickets, a bird and wind
are all the sounds
to be found
deep in green forest
and if another
sound were to be
it would seem
out of place
like me here
in green forest
with pure sounds
and strange thoughts

Jim Crawford

Shock and Horror at Newfound Lake

70 Years Later: A Heroic Tragedy or Unthinking Recklessness?

With no rain and the temperature rising to 84 degrees, the day offers all the promise of midsummer in the Lakes Region. But at pastoral Newfound Lake, a shocking tragedy looms of a scale that will attract nationwide news coverage and front-page headlines in Boston newspapers.

It is Monday, August 5, 1940.

The region is looking forward to the launching of the S.S. Mount Washington II cruise ship on Lake Winnipesaukee, replacing the first Mount Washington that had been destroyed by fire the previous December. In six days, some 10,000 to 15,000 onlookers will send up a roar of applause and cheers as Miss Dorothy Irwin of the Weirs christens the vessel. (Her court of 42 girls from towns in and around the Lakes Region will include Kathleen Emmons of Bristol, Ruth Burbank of Bridgewater and Geraldine Caron of Hebron.)

On the southeast shore of Newfound Lake, local contractor C. Morton Plankey and his workman of 15 years, Martin Keith, are getting a 50-foot-deep well ready for use at a summer cottage owned by Arthur Farineau of Malden, Mass. The well and cottage are located between Lakeside Road – then Route 3A – and the shoreline. Route 3A was then a major north-south corridor heavily used for travel to and from the White Mountains. (The section where the Farineau cottage is located reverted to the quiet residential road it is today after it was replaced by the current alignment further uphill when the highway was reconstructed and upgraded from 1953-1955.)

At the moment, Plankey and Keith are pumping muddy water from the well, which was dug by another contractor the previous fall. Keith, 40, originally from Gorham, had been joined by his wife in their new home in Bristol four weeks earlier.

Plankey and Keith are using a gasoline-driven pump at the surface with a hose reaching into the well. They later lower the pump on a platform some 20 feet into the well to increase the yield as the water level decreases.

All is fine until shortly after noon when the water flow stops, though the gas engine is still running. Keith goes down a ladder to check on it. What he finds isn't clear, but on his return to the top he offers to take a pole down further into the well to measure the water level (which later proves to be about seven feet deep).

The Unfolding of a Disaster

Keith's second descent down the well triggers a horrifying chain of events.

Plankey hears a splash and at first thinks a stone has fallen into the water. However, he gets no response when he calls down to Keith. Plankey twice descends to the bottom of the well and moves his hands and feet around, but is unable to locate Keith. He doesn't realize that carbon monoxide has accumulated in the well from the operation of the gas engine. He feels no personal discomfort, other than his heartbeat is somewhat faster than usual. (Why Plankey wasn't affected by the fumes in the well is never fully understood; doctors later speculate about differences in time and location of the fumes, and in individuals' differing tolerances).

At that point – 1:30 p.m. – efforts to get emergency help begin. Frustration quickly follows.

The Farineau cottage does not have a phone. Someone tries to stop passing cars for help, but the Bristol Enterprise newspaper later reports that "Car after car rushed by without stopping. Finally one stopped and word was sent for aid." Meanwhile, Mary Farineau, the landowner's wife, and her daughter Marjorie rush to nearby Prince's Place, a cluster of cottages at the foot of the lake, and place

47

an emergency phone call from there. Knowing the fire department consists only of volunteers, they then race in their car the two miles to downtown Bristol. They are unable to find any medical or emergency help there, but they do pull the alarm at the fire station (now the home of the Bristol Historical Society) at 2 p.m.

The Ill-Fated Responders

Four men from the volunteer fire department respond: Vernon Tilton, 46, a mechanic and truck driver; Forrest Martin, 41, a mill hand; Albert Paddleford, 50, occupation unknown; and Earl Wells, 23, clerk. Martin and Paddleford are firemen and members of the Rescue Squad. Tilton is a fireman with the longest service of the group – 22 years. Wells is a substitute fireman whose application to become a permanent volunteer for the department is to be acted on the following night.

Wells was married just one week earlier. His wife Louise, who is expecting, is in Laconia today, buying furniture for their new home. Tomorrow is her birthday. Working in his clerk position at Moody's Picture Shop in downtown Bristol, Wells hears the alarms and jumps on the fire wagon as the others pass by enroute to the well site.

Subsequent events will show a critical need for more responders, but other volunteer firemen don't respond, believing that only the Rescue Squad is wanted. But the seven other members of the nine-person Rescue Squad are all unavailable, being out of state or otherwise unreachable, leaving Martin and Paddleford as the only squad members present.

The search for a doctor adds exasperation. The first one contacted is already on another emergency. Some four or five doctors ultimately show up at the site by day's end, but the Enterprise notes that, overall, "Because of the shortage of (responders) and the lateness of their arrival, the delay was distressing and pathetic....To (the people trying to get help) there seemed to be one unavoidable delay after another."

At The Scene

By the time the four firemen pull up at the Farineaus' property the workman, Keith, has been under the water at the bottom of the well for somewhere between a half hour and an hour. The water level is now slowly rising, the pump, motor and platform having been removed from the well by Plankey. At about this same time Everett Merrill, a member of Bristol's Fire Commission, also arrives.

Paddleford is the first responder to descend the ladder into the well. At Merrill's insistence Paddleford has a rope attached to him and carries another. Merrill then leaves to call an ambulance.

There are gas masks on the fire truck, but the men do not use them.

Martin follows Paddleford, carrying a powerful light but not secured by a rope. He and Paddleford succeed in finding Keith and bring him to the surface of the water. They are about to tie a rope around him when suddenly Martin succumbs and drops limply into the water.

At the same moment, Paddleford feels himself losing consciousness. He has one leg entwined around a rung of the ladder in what is known as a "fireman's grip." By shouting or other means (reports vary) he manages to alert those at the top of the well to his distress. They haul both the ladder and Paddleford up.

Paddleford is still breathing. By this time, word of the tragedy has spread and people are hurrying to the scene. Several are medical personnel who happen to be vacationing at Newfound. This includes Nathaniel Sears, a Red Cross instructor from Ashland, Mass. who gives Paddleford artificial respiration. Stable but delirious, Paddleford is driven to Plymouth Hospital. (He is released the next day.)

Wells, then Tilton now descend into the well, one after the other. Neither has a rope or a mask, only a light. Wells has extra motivation to act: Forrest Martin, now lying next to Keith in the water at the bottom of the well, is his brother-in-law, Martin having married Wells' sister.

Both Wells and Tilton are overcome by the deadly fumes and topple into the water. The reactions of those at the top of the well are not recorded, but can be easily imagined. The splashing sound, the stillness that followed and the lack of a response from Wells and Tilton were surely horrifying.

There are now four unconscious and possibly dead men at the bottom of the well.

Chaos and Anger

Up at the surface, confusion soon reigns. All now realize that anyone else who enters the well must have some sort of protection against the deadly gas. In a tragic irony, however, the only people trained in using the gas masks on the fire truck are Paddleford, who was incoherent before being taken to the hospital, and the three firemen at the bottom of the well. All others, including other firemen who have now arrived, have only "haphazard knowledge" of how to use the masks.

An emergency call for assistance goes out to the city of Franklin's fire department. In the meantime, hundreds of onlookers are descending on the scene, including many from several nearby youth camps as well as vacationers from the many cottages in the area. A massive traffic jam has developed on Route 3A, which passes within a few feet of the well, as more people hear of the tragedy and try to get there. For a time, northbound traffic is redirected to the western side of the lake.

Bristol's population in 1940 is only 1,632 (half what it is today). The crowd of firemen, police and local residents now at the top of the well are neighbors and friends of the men at the bottom. They are frantic in their desire to do something – anything – to help the men, but also fearful now that even more will perish if others make the deadly descent. The well is now a terrifyingly mysterious black hole.

The late Nelson Adams, a lifelong area resident who graduated with Earl Wells in the Class of 1936 at Bristol High School, went to the site after hearing sirens. Looking back when interviewed for this article, he said, "Nobody knew what to do."

Nate Morrison, a local farmer, picks up a piece of lumber and threatens to use it against anyone else who dares to try and go down the well. But even he eventually gives in to the desperate desire to do something. He goes partway down the well before being warned that he should have a mask on. He tries on one and is unable to breathe with it. He holds up the mask and asks, "Isn't there one single soul around who knows how to use this?"

Morrison will later excoriate local officials, saying, "No one around the well showed any authority at all." Others agreed. Sears, the Red Cross instructor from Massachusetts, will say, "I saw confusion with no leadership."

Local resident Charles Powden volunteers to go into the well. Morrison and others help him don a mask and give him ropes and a light. Three days later, Powden fought to keep himself under control when he described what he did: "I went down the hole. I saw four dead bodies. (He succeeded in getting a grip on one of the bodies, but was unable to bring it to the surface.) I didn't bring any bodies out. I just wasn't man enough."

Finally, The Rescuers Are Brought Up

Shirley Jewell, a young laborer and volunteer fireman, then goes down with a mask, ropes and a light. He manages to get a rope around Keith, the workman whose collapse triggered the string of tragedies, and brings him to the surface of the well. Keith is unresponsive. Ironically, of the men at the bottom of the well, the one Jewell has brought up has been there the longest by far and likely has the least chance of survival. Martin, Wells and Tilton have been in the well over an hour now.

At that point the Franklin firemen arrive, having raced over the roads 16 miles to the site "in a record run." (Laconia, Rumney, Concord and Plymouth would also send men and equipment) They have better equipment than the Bristol contingent, including a blower, air tubes and inhalators. They quickly retrieve the three men

51

from the well. (The Concord Daily Monitor will offer this blunt report: "The contrast between the quick work of the Franklin group and the heroic but fumbling efforts of local firemen was drawn directly and indirectly by a number of people.")

None of the men are breathing, nor do any have a pulse. "While hundreds of horrified spectators press around the mouth of the well," the men are laid out on blankets a few feet away, alongside Keith. A varied group of medical and fire personnel use artificial respiration and oxygen equipment to try to revive the four men. The group includes Sears and Mary Keenan, a registered nurse from Cambridge Hospital in Massachusetts who, like Sears, is vacationing at the lake.

At 3:30 p.m. a doctor pronounces all of the men dead. Yet those working to revive them keep at it until they finally give up at 6 p.m.

All of the men are found to have water in their lungs. Accordingly, the Medical Referee's official report to the County Solicitor and the State Attorney General gives the cause of the deaths as "Asphyxiation by carbon monoxide and suffocation by water." But the true evil behind their deaths is clear to all. Blood specimens from all of the men show 70 to 75 percent saturation with carbon monoxide. The responding physician states, "If it had been a dry well, all would have died just the same."

The Aftermath

News of the tragedy spread quickly over the wire services. Four men dying in a well was unusual in itself, but the way in which the men went to their deaths – following one another into the well, despite what happened to those who preceded them – undoubtedly sparked added interest. Reports appeared the next day in newspapers nationwide, including the *New York Times*, the *Chicago Tribune* and the *St. Petersburg Times*.

Locally, the shocked residents of the small town of Bristol and the villages surrounding it tried to come to terms with this unprecedented disaster. While all grieved, some angrily demanded answers.

Local farmer Nate Morrison had been outraged at the well site by the fact that no one other than the victims had known how to use the gas masks, and by what he perceived as a total lack of leadership in the efforts to save the rescuers. The day after the tragedy, he sent a petition with 35 residents' signatures on it to the New Hampshire Attorney General stating, "We, the undersigned taxpayers of the Town of Bristol … demand and call for a Coroner's Inquest into the death of four of our citizens …. "

The County's Solicitor and Medical Referee conducted an inquest in Bristol two days later. By all accounts, the hearing was emotionally charged. *The Concord (NH) Daily Monitor's* front-page headline declared, "Witnesses Nearly Hysterical As They Tell Of Deaths of Four In Well At Inquest."

The *Monitor* noted, "[The two hearing officials] sifted through the confused accounts of many witnesses for almost three hours …. At least two of the men who had assisted directly in the futile rescue attempts seemed close to breaking down as they told their tales in low voices."

Morrison was one of several witnesses the hearing officials had to warn to stick to factual testimony. He bluntly related his feelings about lack of leadership, and training in use of the gas masks. His testimony "provided a high point …. His words were received with a buzz of comment from the closely packed selectmen's room which was pressed into service for the inquest.

"Starkest testimony came from Charles Powden [one of the local men who tried to save the firemen], who fought to keep himself under control through the solicitor's interrogation: 'I didn't see anyone down there. All I saw was the hole. Somebody put a rope on me … I went down the hole. I saw four dead bodies. I had the gas mask on, but I didn't bring any bodies out. I just wasn't man enough.'"

In the end, the Medical Referee told the Attorney General that "I believe the whole thing was accidental." The County Solicitor concluded that "Every act at the scene of the tragedy was voluntary and there is no person who could possibly be called the cause of this accident …. in my opinion, there is nothing to present to the Grand Jury."

A Region Grieves

Meanwhile, the Newfound Lake area was in mourning. On the afternoon of the inquest, according to the *Manchester Union*, "Practically the entire town joined in paying tribute to two of the victims, Forrest Martin and Earl Wells [brothers-in-law], for whom a double funeral was held … at the Bristol Baptist church. Places of business were closed during the services." *The Bristol Enterprise* reported that "The Baptist church was far from being of sufficient capacity to accommodate all who desired entrance. Every seat was taken, the standing room in the aisles was crowded, and crowds remained outside."

The day before, Verne Tilton's funeral was held in the Bristol Congregational church; all businesses in the town were closed during his services as well. The funeral for Martin Keith, the workman whose descent into the well led to his death and those of Wells, Tilton and Martin, took place the same day in Gorham, NH, his hometown.

Reactions Are Mixed

Opinions about the tragedy mirrored the conflicted feelings people had about the responders' actions. There was strong sentiment that their bravery deserved admiration. But there was also head-shaking frustration over the deadly risks they took, which some saw as recklessness. The image of one man after another going down into the well, seemingly oblivious to the fate of his predecessors and then, not surprisingly, meeting that same fate, was disturbing. Some even found it embarrassing. The *Bristol Enterprise* came close to admitting as much in an editorial, acknowledging that "Bristol has received some unenviable publicity in this tragic affair."

The *Boston Herald* editorialized that "Although the pressure of excitement and anxiety over the fate of the first man inevitably causes his would-be rescuers to want to act quickly and without thought of their own safety, that impulse should be resisted. It is far better to act cautiously, so that, if the worst happens, only one life will be lost."

The September 1940 issue of *Volunteer Fireman* magazine used the tragedy as a lesson for other firemen nationwide, noting that: "The well at Bristol is typical of numerous dangerous situations in which similar accidents have happened. Manholes, cisterns, silos, and even empty fuel oil tanks, may prove equally deadly …. In making a rescue from such locations the rescuers should think before they act …. It is not natural for a fireman to stand idle when such an accident occurs …. But it may be suicide to enter such a death trap without at least wearing a life line [rope] manned by helpers above who can pull up the wearer at the first sign of trouble."

The author of a Letter to the Editor in the *Concord Monitor* wrote bluntly, "Residents of the Bristol area and witnesses to the tragic incompetence of rescuers will not soon forget the exposition of unpreparedness which they saw on August 5 when four men were uselessly killed …. most amazing of all, not one person in authority knew that when you let a man down into a gas filled area, he probably won't come up unless you have provided a rope by which he may be retracted. The whole management of the emergency was ignorant of the very fundamentals of first aid."

In other Letters to the Editor and in an *Enterprise* editorial, the *Monitor* letter writer was castigated for being insensitive and ill informed: "Isn't there every evidence that no one knew of the existence of gas in the well? … sympathy and praise for the sacrificing efforts of all who tried should be bestowed, and not discouraging criticism … The men who went down into the well and so bravely died, died as you and I might, knowing a friend or relative was to be rescued, and scorning, in the few brief moments necessary to wait for help for themselves, the ropes that were ready. I know that under such circumstances there should be no criticism … I know many members of [fire and police departments] and I know that each, were he placed in a situation such as that which confronted the firemen at Bristol, would do the same as the men who went down into the well."

John Clark was Chief of Police in Bristol until he recently resigned. From his own long experience in law enforcement and that of his father, this tragedy's scenario was no surprise, given the rescue culture that existed in those times: "Back then, there wasn't a lot of training. There was an admiration and fellowship for each other. If you go down in a well, I'm going to come down after you.

"Today, we have better equipment, better knowledge and much better training. If we know something like that (the possibility of gas in the well) is going on or might be going on, we have equipment we can use to test the air before we send someone down. Also, back then, there wasn't a conscious disregard for their own safety, just not a conscious regard for all the issues that could come up. We're much better trained and equipped today."

A Tragedy Best Forgotten?

In researching this article, it was surprising to learn how little this tragedy was acknowledged over the years. At the time, the *Concord Monitor* termed it "the most horrible accident to visit this quiet town in decades." In the 70 years since, no fatal incident in Bristol has equaled the number of lives lost at the well. Yet even those who were directly affected rarely, if ever, mentioned it:

• Mark McSheehy and his wife Barbara now own the cottage where this tragedy occurred. Barbara is the granddaughter of Arthur and Mary Farineau, the landowners in 1940 who hired the well contractor, Morton Plankey. Both Mark and Barbara spent many years vacationing at the cottage with her parents and grandparents, yet until being contacted for this article, Mark says he and his wife "had no clue" that four men had died on the property, or even that a well ever existed there. Nothing about this was ever mentioned to them. (In one of the many ironies to this story, the McSheehys get their drinking water from the popular Breck-Plankey Spring on Route

3A in Bristol. Morton Plankey's descendants allow use of the water by the public.)

• Raymah Simpson, Bristol's Town Clerk and Tax Collector, is the daughter of the late Perley Wells, the brother of Earl Wells. She says she always found it puzzling that the Wells family never talked about this tragedy. The most she ever heard was, "We lost John D [Earl Wells' nickname] in a well." In checking with the Plankey family, Morton's descendants also had very limited, if any, knowledge of what happened.

• The silence extends to documents. A transcript of the inquest was prepared, but no copies exist at the Attorney General's office, the County Attorney's office, or the Bristol Fire or Police Departments. Also, Charles E. Greenwood's *History of Bristol, 1819-1969* makes no mention of this fateful day.

• As for the well itself, it was abandoned, then filled in at some later time. No sign of it remains on the property, nor could anyone contacted for this story pinpoint where it was located. From old news photos, it appears it was somewhere on the south side of the property.

Retrospective

"They should have known that they should not go down into that well." That's the first thought expressed by many in Bristol who recall or were told of this dark day in the town's history. But is that a fair statement? Should that be the bedrock conclusion that underlies every memory of this tragedy?

Granted, the actions of Martin, Tilton, Wells and even Paddleford and Keith can be questioned on several fronts (most importantly, for not using ropes). But also consider this:

(1) Plankey, the contractor, the only person the responders could look to for a situation report when they arrived onsite, had been down the well himself twice (looking for Keith) with no ill effects; he may also have told them that Keith had been down and back up once before his second deadly descent;

(2) Plankey had removed the gas engine from the well by the time they arrived;

(3) Plankey couldn't explain what had happened to Keith;

(4) the ladder was the equivalent of five stories in height; they could have assumed that Keith (or later, their fellow firemen), had simply fallen off the ladder to the bottom due to a misstep or defect;

(5) carbon monoxide is a colorless, odorless, tasteless gas;

(6) as former Police Chief Clark indicated, they were handicapped, compared to today's responders, in knowledge, training and equipment;

(7) the unused gas masks on the truck, had they been used, might well have proven ineffective; unlike the Franklin crew's equipment, there was no way to supply oxygen to them (their apparent effectiveness when Powden and Jewell went down later might instead be explained by the doctors' theories on why Plankey wasn't affected – differences in time and location of the fumes and in individuals' differing tolerances);

(8) by the time Tilton and Wells (the last two to descend) went into the well, Paddleford had been brought up but was in no condition to relate what had happened to him; they only knew that something sinister was afoot, yet they still went down;

(9) Forrest Martin, the first fireman to succumb, was Earl Wells' brother-in-law; add in the bond between all the men and then consider what we would do in their position, standing at the top of the well, getting no response from a relative/comrade, and knowing that we are their last hope.

The image of these four men as lemmings, blindly marching one after the other into a deadly well, has persisted for 70 years. They deserve better. After all, they were trying to rescue others. We weren't able to rescue them. The least we can do is rescue our memories of them.

THE CHILD LEFT BEHIND

Remarkably, for an era when large families were common, three of the four men who died in the well were childless. The fourth, Earl Wells, the youngest of the victims by far at age 23, was looking forward to becoming a father. He and Louise Roby had been married only a week before, and she was expecting.

While grieving, Louise kept a scrapbook in the weeks following the tragic events of August 5, 1940, as a way to honor her lost husband. She placed the many news articles about the well tragedy in it, including all that mentioned her husband.

Seven months later, on March 1, 1941, Louise gave birth to their baby, Earlene Louise Wells, whose first and middle names honor her parents.

Louise died a week later of post-childbirth complications. She was 21.

Earlene Louise Wells was barely a week old and had already lost both her father and mother to sudden deaths.

Fortunately, her maternal grandmother, Florence Roby, took responsibility for raising her.

Now 71 and living in Alexandria with her husband, Richard, Earlene has been forever grateful for Florence Roby's love: "My grandmother was fantastic. When I think back now, she was in her forties at that time, with her own children grown, and for her to take in an infant …."

She says she came to know of the well tragedy gradually. "No one talked about it when I was small. When I got to high school, my grandmother sat down with me one day and gave me the scrapbook my mother had kept."

She looks at the well tragedy objectively: "It was a terrible tragedy. They didn't have the precautions they have now. They did what they were trained to do, but I guess they just weren't very smart about it, especially by today's standards." She never met Albert Paddleford, the lone survivor of the firemen who went into the well. He never contacted her.

Earlene looks back on her upbringing with fondness, thanks in part to the townspeople. "I was looked on as kind of special somehow. I think because of the notoriety, everyone in the town – it was a small town, of course – treated me special. I was actually kind of spoiled."

She smiles when recounting what she learned over the years about her father. "Everyone always called him 'John D', after John D. Rockefeller, I guess because he was a somewhat arrogant, happy-go-lucky guy who always acted as if he owned whatever place he happened to enter." It doesn't surprise her that he jumped on the fire wagon as it passed by the shop where he worked, joining the others on their ill-fated way to the well.

Acknowledgments

Thanks to the Bristol Historical Society for their help, especially Lucille Keegan; to Ron Preble, for the *Volunteer Fireman* article; and special thanks to Earlene Wells, who could not have been warmer or more welcoming during our visits.

Several people helped in the attempt to construct an accurate account of what transpired that day, in the face of often contradictory or misleading news articles (as one example, Martin Keith was, sadly, referred to as Martin Keafe in most accounts appearing the first few days after the tragedy). Two in particular who went to great lengths to help were Nancy Cristiano, Coordinator of the Family Resource Connection at the NH State Library (and Reference Librarian at Plymouth State University's Lamson Library), and Paul Brodeur, Chief Investigator, Criminal Justice Bureau of the NH Attorney General's office. Nancy and Paul, thank you.

Nancy Lincoln

Another beautiful day on Newfound Lake

January: Ice setting up not quite frozen

February: Shanty's are up, people are fishing!

March: Snow, Cold, harsh, strong; and oh so eerily quiet yet inviting

April: Birds are coming back; ice is melting

May: North Winds sweeping down the lake making white caps

June: Water calling and almost warm enough to go in

July: Summer is in Full Swing; fireworks blazing

August: Summer Vacations; family's relaxing

September: Back to school and weekend crowds fewer and fewer

October: Leaf Peepers then nothing!

November: Crisp fall air; delightful hiking

December: Warm with the sun shining and little wind; hints of what's
to come

Building Sand Castles and Memories

5 years old: Not a care in the world beyond this moment
Water: sparkling, lively and full-bodied
Sun: brightly delighting and warming my shoulders
Sand: soft and gentle to the touch

My daughter's blue eyes and laughing so much
Her blond hair ponyed up
Wearing my white T-shirt many times too big
A happy family of three
Building Sand Castles and Memories

Good Lord, what have we done?

Saving a distraught house and buying a dream
Our advantage: internet searching in these economic times
It's a million dollar view on my favorite lake
The price tag is staggering
The taxes are gagging
The house is a mess; neglected and upsetting.

Hard work restoration
My good boy enjoys it
Knows he bought me my dream
Working hard to improve it

He is plumber, exterminator, electrician and then
He learns water fluctuations, dock building and moorings.
We find the chapel delightful, simplistic and pure
We find there are more friends to help us endure

Second thoughts begin to creep in
Correct decision?
Most everything working - but all in fruition?
Main house near our jobs begins to neglect
The once gorgeous lawn is now just a wreck
Feeling pressure and stress
We have our regrets

Then Sara comes driving
Confesses she still cries as she approaches the ledges
Mumma's dream a reality
Future children's destination
Her year-round vacation
Correct decision!

Suzanne Marshall

Day Off

It wasn't his fault.
That rascal jay just jeered at him
while he played in the schoolyard,
cocked its party-hat head,
and in a blue flash
flew off into a bristle of pine.
What could the boy do
but follow him
into the woods?

Overhead
the sun winked through winter clouds,
squeaky-toy birds scolded him,
and dry beech leaves rattled,
fluttering on bare branches
like a fleet of paper kites.

Deer tracks bounded through snow,
half-moon prints edged with ice,
a trail of glass slippers.
What could he do
but follow them deeper
into the woods?

A black flick of tail
caught his eye –
a sleek mink sledding
on its belly

down a steep snow-chute,
slip-sliding, then disappearing
into the stream below.

The stream gurgled and shivered
beneath its crust.
Stalactite crystals hung
from ice-canyon edges,
sparkling in the sun
like a thousand stars.
Who could resist
hurling rock-meteor after meteor,
splintering the air with water and ice?

Can you blame him?
The day just shouted his name –
Come out
and play!

Hebron Sanctuary After the Storm

Grey clouds glower
down on leaf-littered meadow
as mist rises in spectral wisps,
tangles with storm-tossed clouds,
and retreats over distant mountains.
The sun splinters the sky with light.

The wild squawking of jays, jays
from tousled crowns of birch scatter
sprays of raindrops everywhere –
an after-shower.

Two glistening crows stalk the fields,
gawking, bob sleek heads,
listening for the scurry of drowning beetles
while cicadas sear the steamy air.

Through weeping goldenrod and sedge,
elfin frogs spring,
arms and legs bent in prayer,
balance on blades of grass.

Vernal Hymn

spring opens gently

like the breathing in

before a canticle begins

      pale green mist of leaves

      wavers vibrato

      in the crowns of beech

the liquid flute-song

of a single thrush shivers

through slender birch

      veiled fiddleheads bow

      then rise, crescendo

      unfurling song into cool air

the litany of a thousand peepers

trill and swell

ring hallelujah

Jo O'Connor

They say behind every bush in New England there is a spook. With Halloween almost here many New England traditions, like telling spooky stories, and serving tankards of cold apple cider, will no doubt be dusted off and revised in time for the spookiest night of the year!

In keeping with that tradition, and for the fun of it, the story of the Palermo ghost will be retold here along with a couple of other stories native to the New England shores. So grab a tankard and make yourself comfortable.

The ghost of the Palermo Mine story below could be considered a legend. I know the previous owner of the mine. The sea captain story is not exactly legend but I did go to that house looking for a house for us to buy. Apparently a couple of days before I went to look at the "Captain's House" he appeared before another real estate agent and her client needless to say the house was still up for sale. After all, who needs a house where the tenant doesn't pay any rent and scares away guests! According to people who live near Little Big Horn some of the men of the 7th Calvary are not at rest, they have been seen in the area.

Truth or Tricks

Before we begin our journey through the twists and turns of dark tales, there are certain things we must be sure and straight about. First of all, (this comes from good authority), it is not onions you hang on doors or windows to keep the vampires away, but rather string garlic on the portals, at the windows, and around your neck if perchance you dare to venture out on Halloween night. Table salt is a must to banish ghost and goblins, however, when it comes to Irish banshees, you're on your own! And lastly, it would be prudent to have at the ready, a super soaker loaded with ice-cold water, for the tricksters who come sneaking up to your back door!

Ghostly Tales first from the West then to the East

A Haunted Battlefield

It was dark when the mist was rising as Daniel Burton stopped his car on the empty stretch of road that moves cautiously past the area called Last Stand Hill and the monument dedicated to the 7th Calvary. The monument is in memory of Lt. Col. George Armstrong Custer, the 262 Calvary men and the 7th Calvary's Crow and Arikara Scouts who together fought and died during the two-day battle that took place there June 25 and 26 in 1876.

Burton's mind was not on the history of The Little Big Horn when he stopped to rest his road weary bones for a few minutes that night. Instead, he was thinking about the long lonely hours he still had to go before he reached his destination. Neither did he think, as he closed his eyes, that before the night was over he would not be alone.

Daniel was a well-traveled man, a man of caution. Wisely he always kept his car doors locked as he moved about the Country on business. While lock doors can be a good precaution against human interference it's not necessarily helpful when it comes to specters. That is, if you think they exist.

It was the twilight hour, the time between the end of darkness and the beginning of light as the rising mist had become a full-blown dense fog when Daniel suddenly bolted awake. It was the hairs standing up on the back of his neck and the icy chill that ran down his spine that had abruptly awaken him. Through his high beams he saw an outline of something slowly, awkwardly, approaching the front of his car. On lowering his light beams he saw it was the staggering form of a human being. As he watched the silent figure moving closer still Daniel felt his heart beating hard and fast as his mouth suddenly went dry.

69

Too late, Daniel realized he had left his window down. Paralyzed with fear, Daniel was unable to roll up the window and soon the specter, a mortally wounded Lieutenant of the 7th Calvary pressed against his door. He felt the cold breath of the long dead officer on his face as the Lieutenant's head move in the open window and looked intently at Daniel with mournful eyes.

What Daniel saw that night others have said they've seen. Is this story truth or tricks? Who knows? The lesson here could be, don't make any stops anywhere near the Little Big Horn battlefield when it's dark, otherwise, keep the table salt handy!

Tales of Haunts in New England

A Twinkle in a Pirate's Eye:

While it's said, in New England there are spooks behind every bush it also can be said, occasionally there's a spook in a cave or two along the New England Coast. When the moon is at its fullest and the sea is flat along the lower end of the rocky Maine Coast look for her, she waits there, still.

In the seventeen hundreds, pirates from New England tended to their pirating business nearer their homes during the warm months. But pirates preferred the warmer climates in the winter to conduct their business. So before the first snow of a New England winter fell the pirates would set their courses southward towards the warmer Caribbean waters.

Quick, as they called him, was the Captain of the Sea Witch in the mid seventeen hundreds. By all accounts he was a handsome man with the manners of a nobleman who went by another name when he left his ship for the summer months on the rocky shores of Maine.

Norah, her surname is still not mentioned even now, out of respect for her family whenever this tale is told, lived in a village some distant north of Captain Quick's Maine home. She was a lovely young lass, the only daughter of a highly regarded family. As it so happens Norah first trip away from home was to spend that fateful

70

summer with relatives in the village Quick called home. And in the warm days of late spring they met.

It's said the two pledged eternal love on a tiny bit of shore beneath a steep rocky cliff in front of a small but well concealed cave on the last day of summer when the moon was at its fullest and the bitter cold Atlantic Ocean lay flat. On that night he revealed who he really was and that his trip to the Caribbean that year would be his last as the captain of the fearsome Sea Witch. With a solemn promise to return for her, he left that night for the high seas.

So angry was her family when news reached them in the spring that she had given birth to a child they made arrangements to send her and the child to England. But late on the night before she was to leave for England she took her child and little else and fled.

Captain Quick and the Sea Witch were never heard of again. But in the late 20th century a little cave was discovered at the bottom of a sheer rocky cliff on the southern end of the coast of Maine. Inside were the bones of a young woman holding the bony frame of an infant. They lay there still, as they were found.

People from around there say they have seen her standing on that tiny bit of shore holding her infant close when the moon is at its fullest and the bitter cold Atlantic Ocean lays flat. She waits there, still.

A Chilling Sight

There is a quaint little seaside town in Massachusetts where cobble-stone paths, white picket fences, pretty gardens and historical houses are well maintained. It is here in what appears to be a peaceful, unpresumptuous, town lost in time that a long dead Sea Captain once lived. His well-kept, white washed house still stands looking seaward. He was a merchant ship Captain who died in his bed at home in that house. In life this captain had but one fault, he had an eye for the pretty ladies. More than two hundred years later he still has an eye for the ladies!

Over the years many an attractive lady has stepped into his house and has been greeted by the chilling sight of the grinning, sly Captain himself.

Rumors, ghost stories and folklore abound in small New England towns, Groton, New Hampshire is no exception. The story of the ghost of the Palermo mine is a combination of all three. From 1863 to around 1958 the stories coming out of the mines had nothing to do with ghosts. It wasn't until after a crew of miners from N. Carolina came to Groton to work the Palermo and had left three years later did rumors fly.

It seems a young lady from the Rumney area had caught the eye of the "Pit Boss", (foreman or supervisor) during the crew's stay. Soon after the crew left the State, the young lady was reported missing. All searches and inquires turned up nothing as to whether the young woman was alive or dead. And as far as any one knows she never contacted family, friends, or neighbors anytime after her disappearance. One odd thing did occur during the time she was first discovered missing; within the Palermo mine there are three shafts, someone spent two weeks filling in one of those shafts. Who filled in the shaft, and why was it filled in, no one knows even to this day.

Rumors have it that the young lady ran away with the Pit Boss or she was murdered and buried somewhere in the mine. Perhaps this bit of folklore might have been forgotten if it hadn't been for a simple unexpected incident some years later.

In one of the tunnels a visitor happened to have his camera pointing upwards and accidentally clicked a picture. What was seen on the photograph was shocking. In the photo is a ghostly face of a young woman looking down at the visitor! The ghost, they say is the young lady that had disappeared long ago.

On An Odd Year: A Story for Halloween

When the calendar marks the year in an odd number and the leafless branches on the trees sway mournfully in a dark wind and pumpkins have an icy glaze and its Halloween...take care.

In a small northern New England town the story is told about two men who arrived in the Harris Village settlement in 1789. They were unusually tall and broad of chest easily recognizable even at a distant. Brothers they were, Jenkins was their name. They claimed for themselves an entire heavily forested hill, one of the steepest surrounding the village. That these young men lived atop a hill far from village camaraderie and safety and tended to keep to themselves left some villagers speculating about the strangers.

Usually seasons have predictable patterns; however, in 1804 suddenly seasonal weather was anything but predictable. It was strange. Some said a dark hand had cast an evil shadow over the land. First the rains came too early and stayed too long for a good spring planting, and summer brought a devastating drought and the autumn rains did not fill the wells. Then the snow came early and fell deep. The big game once so abundant vanished.

Winter was harsh and hunger moved in to many homes. When more than a few folks discovered some of their provisions and an occasion livestock had turned up missing as the snows deepen, the unsocial Jenkins were suspected. They then became the objects of the vilest rumors.

By spring things were no better and at the end of summer a small band of ill-tempered villagers made their way up the long treacherous path to the brothers' homestead. A man named Holloway led the desperate band, and it was he who first shouted out accusations as soon as he caught sight of the brothers. The brothers tried to convince the men they were innocent but to no avail. Short tempers and empty bellies ignored reasoning and the fight that followed left all of them bruised, bitter and vengeful.

As fall approached an ewe was found dead. Later on a prized milking cow disappeared. And one night a barn burned to the ground. An uneasy, sinister air settled over the Town. People feared the coming winter but most of all they feared the Jenkins. Those fears led a few brave souls to venture under the cover of darkness to spy on the brothers. What they said they had seen was most troubling and very fearsome in deed. The Jenkins brothers were dancing around a bond fire with forms that were transparent that looked like witches and ghouls that were darting in and out of the flames but did not burn. But most frightening of all was the sight of the brothers making things disappear and reappear again.

By mid October the good folks of Harris Village fears grew greater as bitter cold winds stormed the dark nights. Every little creak and moan gave rise to thoughts of unearthly beings moving about. But by the last week in October they became thoroughly alarmed at the news of, Holloway, the man who was the first to confront the Jenkins for all the mischief that had befallen the Town and had led the spying bands up the brothers' hill, had suddenly disappeared.

On the night of October 31, 1805 dark, bare branches swayed mournfully, in the deathly cold wind as all able bodied men and boys who had gathered in the Common, moved silently, stealthily through the Town, past fields where icy glazed pumpkins lay, and on to the path that led to the top of the brothers' hill.

The sudden sound of a hard wood chair scarping across the wide plank floor broke the dead silence in the room startling everyone. All eyes moved upwards as the unusually tall and broad of chest man stood up and started to move apart from the large group sitting in front of him.

"Wait, where are you going? You haven't finished, what happened to the Jenkins?" A voice called out from the group.

"It's Halloween so I thought I'd better start pouring the cider, serve the doughnuts..."

Another voice broke in, "Never mind that stuff, sit down, finish the story." The voice demanded.

Smiling the storyteller gestured towards the back of the room as he said. "How about I let my twin brother finish for me?" Heads turned to the back of the room to see a man stand up who was a mirror reflection of their host. As the twin began to walk towards the front of the room, someone said in a loud indignant whisper. "I don't care who finishes the story, just finish it!"

"I'll do my best to hurry up and finish the story the twin grinned, but first let me formally welcome you all to High Hill Lodge. We, Don and me, Ron Jenkins apologize for our not being here when you arrived this afternoon. While our lodge operates all year long we're here only a few times a year, but we do make a special effort to be here on Halloween."

Don sat down on the chair his brother had vacated and began. "That Halloween night, in the odd numbered year, 1805 when the villagers arrived on top of this hill they found the brothers gone. It was assumed they had seen the lights from the torches moving up the pathway and realizing this time they were greatly out numbered so they ran for their lives."

"Some of the villagers looked for another way down the hill and found one on the back side. They searched that pathway and far into the woods. Those that stayed behind thoroughly searched the two houses, and the barn the Jenkins had built here. To their surprise they found some potatoes, carrots, wild mushrooms, several rabbit skins and little more. There was no sign of butter or cheese or that the missing cow had ever been on this hill. So they rightfully concluded the brothers had not been eating much better then the villagers themselves. But more importantly there was no sign of Holloway, his rifle was not found and nothing resembling a grave was discovered.

That Spring Mrs. Holloway received a letter from New York. Soon after, she sold her livestock, offered her house up for rent or sale, packed up their belongings and she and her children left the Village for good.

At the end of harvest time that year the two brothers were married.

Here Ron paused and instantly questions were raised. "But what of the night when the brothers were seen dancing around the bond fire with spirits and things?" He was asked by another in the audience.

"According to their journals the brothers were celebrating their respective, successful courtships of two ladies in the next village

75

over. And as to spirits, the only spirits those men saw came from their jugs of hard cider."

"Who burned down the barn and what happened to Holloway?" Came two questions, at once.

"There was plenty of speculation after that Halloween night that Holloway had burned down his neighbor's barn and had taken the cow but no solid proof has been found as yet. One thing is for certain; it was Holloway who sent the letter to his wife and children to follow him to New York. There are letters and journals from that time that keep turning up, so maybe we'll eventually know for sure about the barn and cow."

"One more thing, did the Jenkins run when they saw the torches that Halloween night?" Someone in the group asked.

"No they didn't. Back then; it was a day's walk to the other village, more if they had not cut a path on the opposite side of this hill. They had left that morning to visit their future brides."

With no more questions forth coming Ron soon handed each guest a chilled tankard of cider and offered a toast. "Here's to our, great, great, great, great grandfather Benjamin Jenkins, and our, same number of greats, Uncle Thomas Jenkins twin brothers who settled this hill and to all of you, A Happy Halloween!"

Sheila Oranch

A Mother's View

It's a lot different being exhausted than reading about being exhausted. In books they seldom describe the piece of grit in your eye that just can't be gotten out. My neck hurts, my back hurts, and my feet hurt. What did I ever do to deserve this?

He sat there looking like someone had let most of the air and blood out of him. Fine, high cheek bones, downy jaw, and pale blue eyes. A good-looking young man, as my friend used to say he'd turn out to be. But those eyes, like the mind, did not scan or focus. That mind so inclined to flights of bright fancy or wild romance seemed frayed and tattered - almost not there.

We sat opposite him on the couch, my husband, Bill and I. I talked, mostly, and Bill looked worried. Once in a while he would shoot off a burst of logic and practicality, but it couldn't hit such a moving target. "Emotion is all that matters now." I said. Bill looked bewildered and hurt.

This step-child, adopted-child, problem-child, prodigal-son had appeared suddenly at our front door late that night while I was out. Vague, dirty, not asking for anything, just there.

What are you doing with yourself? Do you know what's wrong with your mind? How can we help you if you won't let us? Are you able to understand your condition? How much of your diagnosis do you understand? Does it help to know what the hospital said when something happens that doesn't make sense? Don't you know how much it hurts us when we don't know where you are? Will you try harder to remember to call? What are you planning to do next? We want better than this for you. Try to believe that you deserve care and opportunity in spite of your illness. You don't have to sell out your principles to get what you need. Will you let us help?

He can't focus. It's getting late. I can't focus. It's been a long time since 5:00 AM and too many days, weeks, months since a really good night's sleep. I feel so powerless. Sad and frustrated. We have to go to bed now, no matter what. Maybe he can stay a few days, anyway.

"Have you eaten? Are you hungry?"
"Bill! Haven't you fed him?
"Oh, you were talking..."

No wonder he didn't make sense. He was starved and tired beyond his resources. Walked and hitch-hiked all day. Maybe on drugs, too. I can't tell. I don't have enough information. I tell him, "Eat, shower, sleep and tomorrow we'll talk some more." Tomorrow Bill and I will explore resources of the human services kind. This is a bad time to need help in Massachusetts.

We can only try. And try.

Just Like Home

Glen slouched down the street watching the toes of his shoes make little splashes in the puddles on the sidewalk. He had no particular destination, but wandered on. He just couldn't go home. There was nothing to go home to. There was nothing to go home for.

The argument with Shane that Glen had just walked out on really seemed like the end. There was nothing left for either of them to say. Each had stated a bottom-line viewpoint that sounded non-negotiable. The argument was well-rehearsed. Where could they go from here? The worst part was that all the insulting and degrading things Shane had said about Glen were probably right. He probably was lazy, or why else did he never seem to finish anything? He never failed because he never tried anything difficult or risky. He really didn't have much sense about money, and consistently spent money on impulse to make himself feel better (or to try to butter up Shane). The apartment was a mess, the rent was past due, and the deadline for his next story was approaching fast.

"Why can't I finish that damn story?" he whined half out loud. "Why is life so unfair?" Glen drifted into his habitual pastime of reviewing all his woes. Shane was paying more attention to her job than to him. Not so long ago, it seemed, they had been totally wrapped up in each other, happily making all sorts of romantic plans. They moved in together, and that had been wonderful...for a while. Then the novelty had begun to wear off, and the little quirks had started to wear on. Glen had gradually slipped into constant negativity, and the most Shane could get out of him when she got home from work and asked how the writing was going, was "Not great. You know, if we only had more space (or a better word processor, or ...) I could really work." He managed to write some things, and some got published. He sold enough to almost pay the rent: articles for trade publications, promotional pieces for small businesses, and an occasional "true romance" story. Not what he wanted to write. Not well-crafted gems of short stories, or well-developed chapters of his novel. He felt like a failure, and much of the time he acted like a loser. Shane was pulling farther away and beginning to wonder if Glen's "slump" (as he called it) was actually temporary after all. If he didn't snap out of it soon, he would lose his lover, his apartment, likely his chance to make it as an artist. It seemed like his life was about to go down the tubes, and everything he did just made things worse.

And then there was his agent, who didn't get him any jobs. What Glen really needed was a fat advance to live on so he could write the "real stuff" without being constantly dragged down by hacking for a living. Matt kept insisting that no publisher would give him a contract without seeing a reasonable chunk of the proposed book. But Glen couldn't get it together to write under such adverse circumstances. Why wouldn't they just accept a brief sample with an outline, and have faith in his talent? Matt wasn't working hard enough for Glen. Maybe he needed a new agent.

Worst of all, Glen's mother kept nagging him to get a "real" job. She didn't understand that his creativity was all he had. Sometimes Glen wondered if he had chosen to be a writer by default, because he wasn't competent to do anything else. He had not taken any "useful" courses in college (except typing), and certainly had not learned anything career-related in high school. He was not particularly strong or coordinated, and hated any kind of selling. He had waited tables summers during college, and hated that. He had no interest in money for its own sake or diddling with numbers all day. He did have a way with words, but too often had nothing that seemed very important or interesting to say. Glen felt caught between a rock and a hard place. The only thing he was halfway good at wasn't getting him anywhere.

If only he could get a break, be noticed, discovered, scooped up by a talent scout or kindly editor, Glen just knew he would make good. No, he would be great! If only he had a chance. But luck was elusive. Glen waited in ambush. What he needed was a little recognition as a way to build his self-confidence and settle some of his doubts. The world would only know him through his work, but for now all he could project was frustration, self-pity, and depression.

His novel was going nowhere, and for weeks he had been hung up on a damn romance story. He felt as though this story captured the essence of his life—a brilliant idea that eluded focus and would not ripen to a spectacular conclusion. It had to have a spectacular conclusion, so he could get published, and noticed, and have his fortune made. The fortune was essential. His landlord was getting aggressive. Time was running out.

Glen's consciousness surfaced from his well-worn wallow, and he noticed that he was on an unfamiliar street. There were little stores scattered among the brownstone houses, and the names on the stores were exotic. He tried to place the culture, but couldn't. Some looked vaguely familiar, maybe European or old-fashioned. There weren't many people out on the street, and it was starting to get dark. Glen realized that he was hungry, cold and tired. But the way things had been going lately, he did not have much money to spend on luxuries like restaurant food. It did, however, seem like a long way home. Looking farther down the street, Glen saw a small neon sign and, turning that way, he read "Just Like Home." The entrance was down a few steps, and the facade was modest, so he figured the prices might be within his reach. As he pushed through the red wooden door, a comforting smell of fresh baking dissolved his doubts. The place smelled just like Glen had always thought home ought to smell, although, he thought resentfully, his never had.

As he started across the room towards a table in the corner (so as to have a wall at his back—a gunfighter's trick he learned from television), a small round woman with red cheeks intercepted him. "No, no, Dear, you sit right here in the middle. There is no one here more important than you. You should have the nicest place to eat."

Glen took a breath to argue, but the hostess had already pulled out a chair and was cheerily patting the seat to encourage him. He shrugged and sat. After all, there was nobody else in the room for him to keep track of anyway. The chair had a seat cushion that looked hand-embroidered. It was very comfortable. His hostess had bustled out into the kitchen and came back with a glass of papaya juice. She set it on the table by Glen's plate, and murmured,

"The bathroom is over there, if you'd like to wash up, Dear. Dinner is almost ready." Then she hustled back into the kitchen.

Glen sat and held his breath for a minute, and wondered how the lady knew he liked papaya juice. It occurred to him to be insulted that she had seemed to be hinting that his hands were dirty, but then he thought they probably were and went to wash them.

When he returned, a small bowl of soup and a round, crusty French roll waited at his place. Since he had not been given a menu, Glen began to worry that he had stumbled into one of those quaint, expensive little restaurants that sometimes hide in down-fallen neighborhoods waiting to be "discovered" by the gentry. He resolved to get the prices when the next course came out. And anyway, since they hadn't given him a menu or posted any prices, if he couldn't afford the meal it was THEIR fault, not his. If they ended up losing money on the deal, it would teach them something about doing business in America. Meanwhile, it would be a shame to let this aromatic broth get cold. The roll was still warm when he broke it open, and the butter was just soft enough to spread. Glen was in heaven. Very seldom had he gotten any food served first, being one of several children, and most often his bakery purchases were day-old at the thrift shop. He began to relax and enjoy his food.

Just as Glen was mopping the last of the soup with the last crust of roll, he heard the kitchen door swing open and the same woman, hands swaddled in a towel, brought over a large covered container with steam leaking out around the edges. Glen spoke quickly and somewhat angrily, before she could uncover the dish. "Madam, please. You haven't bothered to show me a menu, and I wasn't planning to eat out so I didn't bring much money with me. The soup was fine, and that really would be enough. I don't want any trouble." He had some trouble finishing his little speech, though, because the smell from the dish was incredible.

"Oh, dear me! Don't worry at all. All I want is for you to be pleased. We never ask more than a person can give. You just enjoy your dinner, and we'll talk about it later."

"Uh, I, uh, well, if you say so." Glen's resolve had by this time been totally eroded by the tantalizing smell, and he was too hungry to think very far ahead. The lady lifted the cover off the dish, and Glen saw a remarkable array of casserole, green vegetable, and apple sauce neatly displayed on a dish with little ridges between each of the kinds of food. Out of a fold of the towel, another crusty roll appeared. She scampered into the kitchen and brought back a tall, cold glass of milk.

"Now, isn't that nice?" she queried. "You just eat your dinner, and I'll have a surprise for you when you're all done." She smiled serenely at him, and retreated to the kitchen. By the time she had taken two steps, Glen was already on his second bite of casserole. He wasn't sure what was in it, but that didn't seem to matter at all. The vegetable was cooked just right, and cut into bite-sized pieces. The apple sauce tasted home-made. Glen lost all ability to worry, or even think, and just ate slowly and lovingly until everything was gone. As he was scraping the last bit of sauce from the plate, his hostess emerged with a small plate in one hand, and two mugs in the other. She put the plate and one mug in front of Glen, and sat down with the other mug in front of herself.

"Here, let me move this dirty dish. There, now you try your dessert, and let me know how you like it. I made it up fresh for you." She lifted her eyebrows expectantly.

Glen poked his fork into the domed pastry, and a cloud of fruit-scented steam escaped. He had thought he was satisfied, but this smell brought out a ravenous hunger unlike anything he had ever experienced. Now this was heaven! The temptress watched, smiling broadly as he quickly gobbled her offering. As he finished, he noticed the mug filled with hot chocolate, just cooled enough to drink. He sighed, pushed back his plate, and cuddled the mug.

"Now. I am really going to have to find out how much all this costs," he grated in an aggrieved tone. "I may end up washing dishes for you for a month!"

"Is that what you do for a living?" she asked gently. "I think a bright, young man like you must do something very important. Probably something creative. What do you do?"

"What I do and how I make a living are not necessarily the same things." Glen sighed sadly. "I write, but so far I have not made much money at it. I'm beginning to think I am doomed to be a real failure." Glen was so distracted by self-pity that he forgot to pursue his question. The woman made soothing tsk, tsk noises and waited patiently for Glen to continue. He couldn't resist a sympathetic ear. Out poured the inventory. He described in gruesome detail all the indignities heaped on him by an uncaring society. The final insult, he griped, was that he felt betrayed by his own subconscious. The present doldrums in his writing could not be accounted for by any changes in his circumstances, so he could only believe that he suffered from a perverse inner need for failure. If he couldn't trust his own mind, who could he trust? He might as well get a job washing dishes. At least if he worked in a restaurant, he would probably get enough to eat!

All the time Glen was speaking, his hostess had listened, nodding occasionally, and looking appropriately sad or indignant as each point was expressed. She seemed truly moved by Glen's recital, and shook her head slowly as she appeared to think about it.

"It doesn't seem fair, does it? You, with so much talent, and nothing going right for you. I bet you could write very nice stories if you just got a few breaks. If only people would treat you right. If only things weren't so hard..."

Glen's eyes filled with tears. People never seemed to understand. How good it felt to have someone give him some sympathy! Now he really felt sorry for himself. He felt like he should just give it all up and do something easy. Something ordinary with obvious steps and standards. He closed his eyes and sank into a soft, gray funk.

The woman stood up and patted Glen on the shoulder. "There, there. It'll be all right. I think it's too late for you to go home, so you just stay in one of our guest rooms. We keep them ready just in case, and you're the only one we have to pay attention to tonight. No arguments, now, you just relax and enjoy yourself. I'll have one of the girls come and get you in a minute."

Glen hadn't noticed before, but the hostess seemed to be better dressed than he expected a waitress to be. He thought she must be the owner or the owner's wife. Who were "the girls?" If there were other employees, why hadn't one of them served his dinner? Maybe she was referring to one of her children. He was confused. But the big meal had made him sleepy, and he couldn't seem to focus on a question. Maybe he had been drugged and they were going to rob him. It would serve them right that he had so little to lose. There didn't seem much point in fighting with her, and he was so depressed anyway, that it was hard even to care about his personal safety. They would just have to work it out in the morning. Maybe he would be washing dishes for a month. But if he got to eat the food, that wouldn't be so bad.

There was a little noise behind him, and Glen turned to see a young woman enter through a draped archway he hadn't noticed before. All he could do was stare at her, because she was very pretty and dressed in what looked like a pink prom dress. In fact, she reminded Glen very much of the picture in his childhood book of "Cinderella." She smiled, gave a little dip of her head, and said, in a soft voice, "Will you come with me?"

"Uh. Uh. Sure. I guess so. Uh. Thank you," was all Glen managed, as he awkwardly pushed back his chair and stood up. The girl (she seemed quite young) smiled again and held back the curtain. Not knowing where he was going or quite why, Glen stepped through the archway and a few steps beyond. He seemed to be in a foyer, but the light was too dim to make out details. There was a curved, open staircase with a wooden bannister on his left, and another archway on his right. The layers of filmy fabric of her dress rustled as his guide glided toward the staircase. As she passed him, she smiled up into his eyes and brushed her hand along his arm.

"Your room is this way. I know you'll be comfortable. We do want to please you." She started up the stairs. Glen was feeling warm. He really began to wonder what this place was all about. This girl looked as sweet and innocent as anyone's sister, but she acted like they shared some kind of secret. If she had any ideas of getting him in trouble, she could forget it. He wasn't going to fall for that kind of adolescent maneuvering. With some determination, but not much fortitude, Glen followed her up the stairs. As the stairs curved he had a view of more of the area they were leaving, and noticed that the furniture and draperies looked like expensive antiques, but not in very good taste (by modern magazine standards). What was this place?

The second door on the left was open, and Glen stepped cautiously in to find the girl in pink taking some things out of a dresser drawer.

"Here are some things for you to wear. The bathroom is over there. You get comfortable, and I'll be back in a little while to see what you need," she said, as she slipped out and closed the door.

Glen looked around the room. There was a high brass bed with a plush spread, a dresser, a small table, and two chairs. The wallpaper was pinkish beige, and over the table was a small picture. Glen took a closer look, and thought he recognized the scene. It reminded him of one of the frequently used sets of his favorite cowboy show when he was a kid. The stories always were supposed to be set in different towns, but he noticed pretty young that the same fake boulder showed up in a lot of episodes. Presented this way as a picture, he thought perhaps the set had been copied from the original painting. But then he wondered if the painting was copied from the television set. He didn't know enough about art to tell if this was a real painting or a print, or even a paint-by-numbers picture, but it made him feel very much at home.

He realized after a few minutes that he was only semi-conscious, and should probably get ready for bed before he fell asleep standing there. And the girl had said she would be back. He didn't want to be caught half-dressed when she arrived. He gathered up the things she had put out for him, and went into the bathroom. The fixtures were gold (probably actually brass), and the towels were thick. The clothing turned out to be pajamas and a dressing gown. Glen was not used to sleeping dressed, but thought in this situation it would be diplomatic to do so. There were toiletries available, so he used them, too. After all, no matter how much the dinner had cost, he was now an invited guest and it would be ungracious to reject hospitality. He liked the luxuries as much as the next person, and hoped someday to live like this all the time.

As he stepped back into the bedroom, the hall door opened and the girl, wrapped in some kind of flowing robe, glided in carrying a tray with two glasses and a cut-glass decanter. She nudged the door shut with a sinuous movement of her hip and put the tray down on the table. She switched off the lamp, leaving only the light from a pair of wall sconces which fractured into little rainbows as it passed through the facets on the decanter. She sat in one of the chairs and motioned Glen to the other. Warily, he sat down and stared at her. She smiled conspiratorially, and poured a golden liquid into each of the glasses.

"Uh, are you sure you're old enough to drink?" Glen semi-whispered.

"I am old enough to do anything I want to do. Or maybe even that you want me to do," was her silky-voiced reply.

Glen swallowed dryly and took a timid sip of his drink. His companion smiled and nodded approvingly, then also sipped from her glass. Whatever this drink was Glen loved it. He felt a knot of tension dissolve somewhere deep inside himself, and realized that although he had been tired and sluggish, he had not really been relaxed. In fact, he thought possibly he had never been really relaxed as long as he could remember. His shoulders began to ease out of their habitual defensive clench, and he sighed deeply.

"There, that's better," the girl said and Glen jumped a little, because he had been drifting off in a golden mist. She reached out and touched his arm gently. "You must have a lot on your mind. Let's forget about all that. I'll give you a backrub, and we can get to know each other better. My goal is to help you to relax."

"I'm barely able to stand up already," Glen muttered, but having come this far, and having resigned himself to fate for this odd evening, he picked up his glass and sipped some more. A warm glow diffused through his insides, starting with the top of his head and ending somewhere just below his navel. This stuff was good! Delicately, but determinedly, Glen kept sipping. Any doubts or hesitations he had clung to melted as surely as spring snow.

The girl just smiled and sipped her drink.

Glen started wondering what the backrub would be like, and how he would react to being touched by a beautiful stranger. He'd probably fall asleep and insult her, but that was her problem. She was the one who wanted him to relax.

Looking at her now, Glen thought this girl could not be as young as he first thought. She had an air of assurance that he suspected only came with experience. Maybe she was some kind of actress. Whatever she was, and why ever she was paying so much attention to him, he was certainly enjoying himself.

"Come here, now. This is going to feel good," she said as he drained the glass. She took his arm gently and led him to the bed.

As he turned to ask her how to position himself, she began to take off his robe and pajamas. Glen was too surprised to do anything, and by the time he had gathered his wits, she had him stripped to pajama bottoms. She then pushed him backwards, and he sank onto the bed.

"Now you just cooperate, and I'll take care of everything," she said as she rolled him onto his stomach and began slowly kneading his shoulder muscles.

Glen went limp. This woman seemed to know where every muscle that had ever hurt was located. As the aches drained out, a tingling crept in. Instead of falling asleep, Glen began to feel strangely energized. As he started to roll over to thank her for her ministrations, she slid onto the bed beside him and locked him in a hot, demanding kiss.

Without further thought, Glen responded to the invitation fervently.

Some while later, Glen woke up with the feeling that something was different. He felt someone beside him in the bed, and turned to look. The woman who had "relaxed" him so completely was leaning on her elbow watching him. She reminded him of someone, but he couldn't quite place the face. She seemed older than he had believed, but after all, he was now in a position to examine her quite closely.

"There now, isn't that better?" she crooned.

Glen did feel better. In fact, he felt terrific. He wondered what, if anything, he could do for her. He smiled, and started to say just that, but she spoke first.

"I hear you're a writer."

"Yeah. At least that's what I'm trying to be," he muttered.

"Would you write me a story? I mean, would you write a story with me in it? I think in a story I could he anything a man needed. What do you think of that?" she tilted her head and looked at him sideways.

"I think you're doing a pretty good job of it in reality!" Glen blurted out.

"Good. That's just what I'm here for. Come here." She wrapped herself around Glen and he forgot about talking.

What may have been moments or hours later, Glen awoke and felt that funny sense of difference again. He turned sideways, but was alone in the bed. He looked around, and over by the table his lover was sitting in one of the chairs and pinning her hair up. The position and gesture struck him as piercingly familiar. He realized that she reminded him of his mother. But it was his mother as she must have been when he was very young. She also had been beautiful, but children and hard times had aged her quickly. By the time Glen was old enough to pay attention to what adults really looked like, his mother had been worn down to a gray nub. She had had little energy left for her needy fourth child.

Glen's eyes closed, and he drifted back to sleep. He felt cold. He looked around and found himself in an empty gray room. There was nobody else around, and it felt like nobody had been there for a long time. Glen didn't know why he was there all alone. He was cold and uncomfortable. He wondered if anyone would ever come there again. There was no door. There was no window. Glen's heart began to beat faster. He was afraid that he would be in the gray room forever, just cold and lonely, and probably wet and hungry, too. He began to cry and call for his mother, but she didn't come.

Glen became angry that his mother did not come when he needed her so much. Why didn't she care for him? She went when the baby cried. What was wrong with him that she did not love him as much as the baby? Nobody came. Why didn't anybody care? Glen was cold and lonely and frightened and angry. He ran around the room and beat his head against the walls and screamed. He thought if he ran against the wall as hard as he could, maybe he would crash right through and find his mother. He yelled as loud as he could and ran straight at the wall. Glen sat up in a cold sweat with a vivid memory of waking up from a bad dream at the age of two or three and screaming for his mother. She had been in another room, and called out to him in a muffled voice, "Glenny, what's the matter? Did you have another bad dream? Mommy's here, but I can't come to you right now. Go back to sleep. Please go to sleep, Dear. Mommy's here..." Then a man's voice, his father's, blurred and angry-sounding, said something Glen couldn't quite understand. His mother responded in a cajoling tone, and his father, who Glen now realized was drunk, said loudly, "He'd better shut up and stop bothering us! I swear I'll kill that kid if he has one more of those damn dreams."

Glen had felt abandoned. Unloved and unprotected. Ashamed that he had wakened his poor, tired mother (and maybe the baby, as well). Terrified that the unpredictable, violent-tempered man who seemed to control his mother would actually kill him if he suffered another bad dream. He wondered how he could stop his dreams, and became afraid to go to sleep at night. He began to dread those nights his father actually made it home, and sometimes shut himself in his closet in case he fell asleep and had a dream. Glen's waking life became almost as grim and frightening as his dreams, until his father stopped coming home at all. His mother cried a lot for a while, but the household gradually settled into a fearful calm. They never found out what had happened to him. They lived in desperate poverty, as his mother tried to keep the family together.

As an adult looking back, Glen could sympathize with his mother, who probably had just gotten the baby to sleep and had to get up in a few hours, and needed to appease an unreasonable and abusive husband. As a child, he had only felt self-pity, anger, and fear. Now his mother was a bitter, controlling person who was never satisfied and always wanted more attention than he could give her.

Just as he was gearing up to feel really sad and pitiful, Glen looked over and saw that he was once again the sole object of this woman's attention. She was watching him with a fond smile, and when she caught his eye she immediately got back into the bed. As he started to explain what he had been thinking, she put a finger to his lips and pulled his head down to her breast. Then she patted him on the shoulder and held him very close and still. Glen felt a lump rise in his throat, and softly, unexpectedly, he began to cry. He wept almost silently, but held tightly to the arms that cradled his head. Huge racking sobs came up, and he felt as though he would be torn apart except that the gentle arms held him together. After a while he ran out of tears, sighed and collapsed weakly.

Glen looked up, eyes swollen from crying, and started to apologize. His companion put her hand on his forehead and pressed him down onto the pillow.

"It's OK. I understand. Everything is going to be all right. You rest, now, but don't forget to write that story."

Glen felt his eyes closing. He wanted to talk to her, to explain his behavior, to thank her for being there for him, and say that now he understood where much of his negativity came from, but he just could not stay awake.

The next thing he knew, Glen was waking up with sunshine spreading through the room. There was a coffee service and bowl of fruit on the table, and his clothes were neatly folded on the chair. He went into the bathroom, washed and got dressed. He sat down and poured a cup of coffee, and saw a note on the tray. In elegant script it read, "You can't always get what you want, but if you try, sometimes you find just what you need." He smiled. He had the germ of an idea that as an adult he could learn to comfort himself. That he could choose to have people in his life with the time and energy to pay attention when he was sad. That Shane cared a lot for him, but just couldn't stand his constant complaining. All she needed was a chance—just like him.

Glen shook his head. He did not even know that woman's name, but he knew he was loved. He would write her story. But first he would finish the story he had already started. And as he thought about that, several more ideas came rushing into his mind. He wrote himself some reminders on the back of the note, and put it in his pocket. It might be quite a while before he had time to write her story, but someday he would do it for sure.

As he came down the stairs into the ornate lobby, which in daylight looked a bit older and dustier, Glen saw the woman from the restaurant sitting at a little secretary desk in the corner. She seemed to be filling in some kind of form. She looked up and smiled as he approached, and handed him a dinner check. His first impulse was to start making excuses, but as he looked at the bill the words stuck in his throat.

"$13.50! Is that all? For everything you've done for me? I don't believe it."

"No, Dear. That is for the dinner. You've only gotten what you needed and what you deserved. Call it a gesture of good will. Someday you'll be rich and famous, and we can look at your success, and say we knew you when. And anyway, everybody likes to be appreciated, and you are such a good eater!"

Glen dug into his battered nylon wallet and handed her the money, which was all he had.

"Now you run along and get to work. We're looking forward to your stories."

With that she hustled Glen out and shut the door. Glen stood on the steps and looked up at the street. The previous night's rain had washed away the smoke and pollution. The sun was shining. Life was full of potential, and Glen was full of energy. Nobody owed him anything, but as of today, he knew he was going to get it all. He hopped up onto the sidewalk and trotted towards home. About halfway down the block, Glen looked back to set the location of "Just Like Home" in his memory, but he could not make out which building it was in without the neon sign. He shrugged and kept going. If he ever needed it again, he was sure he would find it. But the way he felt now, he probably never would.

Juliet Elizabeth Pruden

Un Encuentro Al Azar—A Chance Encounter

Una noche prestada
Cayó después de la puesta del sol reluciente
El cielo lleno de nubes tempestuosas
Las dos barcas meneadas en el lago sosegado
Para ti, una aventura nueva
Para mi, un regalo que compartir

A borrowed night
Fell after the glittering sunset
The sky filled with stormy clouds
Two boats wiggled into the still lake
For you, a new adventure
For me, a gift to share

Movimos en silencio de la playa
Nos deslizamos por el crepúsculo
Hasta que el río nos rodeó
Y los árboles alargaron las ramas
Intentando seducirnos dentro de su apretón
No nos acercamos, había peligro

We moved in silence from the beach
We slipped through the twilight
Until the river surrounded us
And the trees stretched out their branches
Trying to seduce us into their grasp
We didn't get too close, it was dangerous

No hablamos
Solamente escuchamos la canción placentera
Ya que los grillos tocaban las piernas como
violinista
Y las cigarras canturreaban el bajo
Pasamos rozando el agua como los insectos
acuáticos
Tampoco no nos zambullimos

We didn't speak
Just listened to the pleasant song
 As the crickets were playing
their legs like a violinist
And the cicadas hummed the bass
We glided across the water like
aquatic insects
Neither did we dive in

Ha pasado un año.
Como la lechuza que vuela arriba,
Somos más sabios, más pacientes,
más comprensivos
Me sigues por la oscuridad
Me fias de navigar el sendero aguachento
Pero ¿tenemos fe en nuestra amistad?

A year has passed.
Like the owl that flies overhead,
We are more wise, more patient,
more understanding
You follow me through the darkness
You trust me to navigate the watery path
But do we have faith in our affinity?

Solamente sé que la vida es más rica,
La música más dulce,
y hay más momentos mágicos
cuando estamos juntos.
Las llaves permanecen debajo de la luna
Sobre el carro, alrededor las curvas
De las montañas al oír los tangos apasionados.

I only know that life is richer,
The music sweeter,
And there are more magic moments
When we are together.
The keys remain beneath the moon
on top of the car, around the curves
Of the mountains upon hearing the passionate tangos.

Con los pies en el lago tibio,
Escondidos por la noche,
Las nubes desaparecen
Y mano a mano,
Atestiguamos la estrella fugaz.

With our feet in the warm lake,
Hidden by the night
The clouds disappear
And hand in hand,
We witness the shooting star.

No puedo definir con palabras nuestra conexión
Ya no sé porque nos encontramos
Solo que, quizas no sea por nosotros decir,
Simplemente ser
Me alegre de que estés aquí
Y te echaré de menos hasta que
Un otro año haya pasado
Raro amigo mío

I can't define with words our connection
I still don't know why we found each other
Only that, perhaps it's not for us to
say, simply to be
I'm glad that you're here
And I will miss you until
another year has passed
_____ friend of mine

I am choosing not to translate the word raro. It encompasses many applicable meanings in Spanish, but to try to choose just one in English doesn't fit. Lo siento.

El Camposanto~~The Burial Ground

Debajo del manto del invierno blanco,
Afuera en el viento crudamente feroz,
Bajo las flores secadas, en estado latente,
Sepulté lo que nos juntamos
Después de huyó en Septiembre.

Beneath the cloak of winter white,
Outside in the harshly fierce wind,
Under the dried flowers, dormant,
I buried what joined us together
After it fled in September.

El destino, la magía, la sorpresa,
El misterio, la gloria, la esperanza,
Transformaron a la fatalidad.
Y por tu silencio, no te perdonaré.
No en este tiempo.

Fate, magic, surprise,
Mystery, glory, hope,
Turned to doom.
And for your silence, I will not forgive you.
Not this time.

Soy más fuerte que puedas saber.
Soy intrépida guerrera sola.
No puedo soportar tu cobardía ni punto débil.

I am stronger than you can possibly know.
I am an intrepid warrior alone.
I cannot abide your cowardice nor
your weakness.

Confié en ti y fue un idea falsa;
Creer que yo pudiera contar contigo.

I trusted in you and it was a false notion;
Believing that I could count on you.

Pero la diferencia es que por este resultado,
Llego a ser más abierta a darme el gusto
De compartirme verdaderamente
Con alguién especial.
Mientras que te protejas,
Cueste lo que cueste.
¡Tan atemorizado!

But the difference is that as a result,
I become more open to allowing the
sensation of truly sharing myself
With someone special.
While you protect yourself,
At all costs.
So afraid!

Acepté un riesgo, y me mejoró.
¡Qué lástima que no puedas hacer lo mismo!
¿Nunca quieras realizar todas tus posibilidades?

I took a risk, and it improved me.
How sad that you are unable to do the same!
Do you never want to realize your
full potential?

Quizás después de derreta el manto de nieve
En el jardín,
Igualmente pueda tu corazón,
Y los brazos en que te enrollas protectoramente
Aun durante el sueño,
Empiecen desplegar como las hojas nuevas.

Perhaps after the blanket of snow in
the garden melts,
So too can your heart,
And your arms in which you wrap
yourself protectively, even in sleep,
May begin to unfurl like new leaves.

Cuando las flores prosperan
Sobre nuestros restos,
Esperaré un caballero verdadero, sin armadura,
Sin escudo,
Que sin miedo extende la mano.

When the flowers bloom
Over our remains,
I will await a real knight, without
armor, without a shield,
Who fearlessly reaches out his hand.

Doug (Amoo) Riddle

Village Stones

Hebron Village is OH SO PRETTY,
Tucked far away from the nearest city.
There's a green common, a quiet place,
Between each home is ample space.
A gazebo adorns the village center.
With an academy and able mentors
It's so nice we're sure you'll like it.
I lot of people choose to bike it.

But, once or twice as visitors came,
They left behind their marks of shame.
They took from gazebo's border of stones,
And littered the common like broken bones.
When Marie came the grass to mow,
Her blade hit stone and it did throw
It right at Suzy, who happened nearby,
And hit that child close by her eye.

Doctor Bob sewed Suzy with several stitches.
She was heard to say, "Oh my, it itches."
What a shame this thoughtless crime,
Had to ruin sweet Suzy's recess time.
And I am certain the rotary mower,
Turns a trifle uneven and a whole lot slower.
The damage remains, cause it's not so simple,
And Suzy, our lass, wears an extra dimple.

Independence Day

Did you ever pause or wonder why,
It always rains on the fourth of July?

The day arrives and the Morn breaks clear.
It's just after breakfast the dark clouds appear.

When the folk arrive and the picnic is set,
Sheets of water come down wet, wet.

The hamburgers are soggy and the hot dogs are limp.
It would have been better if we had live shrimp.

The fireworks planned to cap the event,
Must wait a day before skyward they're sent.

And, brighten our spirits with ohs and ahs.
We are so lucky this country is ours.

Our forefathers gave us a land that is free,
But it might have been drier on two, five or three.

Independence Day comes but once every year.
So smile sweetly and be of good cheer.

Forget your damp and downhearted thinking.
Raise your glass, and a toast be drinking.

No matter what the weather on this special day,
Join me in shouting hip, hip, hooray!

I'm Drinking From My Saucer

I've never made a fortune and it's probably too late now.
But I don't worry about that much, I'm happy anyhow.
And as I go along life's way, I'm reaping better than I sowed.
I'm drinking from my saucer, because my cup has overflowed.

Haven't got a lot of riches, and sometimes the going's tough.
But I've got loved ones around me, and that makes me rich enough.
I thank God for his blessings, and the mercies He's bestowed.
I'm drinking from my saucer, 'cause my cup has overflowed.

O, remember times when things went wrong, my faith wore
somewhat thin.
But all at once the dark clouds broke, and sun peeped through again.
So Lord, help me not to gripe about the tough rows that I've hoed.
I'm drinking from my saucer, 'Cause my cup has overflowed.

If God gives me strength and courage, when the way grows steep
and rough.
I'll not ask for other blessings, I'm already blessed enough.
And may I never be too busy, to help others bear their loads.
Then I'll keep drinking from my saucer, because my cup has
overflowed.

George and Now

The father of our country
Was a man of comely grace.
Over six feet tall, straight of back,
Somewhat plain of face.

They bled him to make him well.
And imbedded his teeth in lead.
Without such tender, loving care,
He still might not be dead!

His doctor, and his dentist,
I'm sure they meant his cure,
But the manner that they treated him
Was very, very poor.

He never told a lie!
We've all been told that's so,
Why don't other politicians?
Find that the way to go?

Carpet Stains

The little boy carried a huge ice cream sundae,
Big enough to last from Saturday to Monday.
It had syrup and nuts and was covered with jimmies.
His sister was heard to express her loud "gimmies"

As he walked to the door off his treat came a drop,
From his spoon to the floor chocolate syrup went plop.
He stooped to retrieve it and down came his spoon
Loaded with ice cream. It occurred about noon.

He looked at the mess and saw what he'd wrought,
To clean it up was his very next thought.
He bent over quickly to wipe it, I'd say,
As his sundae from plate went slip sliding away.

Our little hero, it's noted, kept true to his chore,
And scrubbed his sundae all over the floor.
Carpet stains remind us we all could be thinner
If we waited for dessert 'til after our dinner.

Bear, A Black Lab Retriever

The Kanines lived in a little house,
Just right for them and perhaps a mouse.
There was Dad who's name was Dan,
And Olive was their mother,
A brother George who always ran,
Sister Susan and one other . . .
Bear, a Black Lab Retriever.

Dan made his living as a clerk.
And Olive was a diligent soda jerk.
George was expected in school each day,
and loved it like no other.
Thick glasses sharpened Susan's way,
As they did her father, mom and brother.
Bear was a Black Lab Retriever.

Bear was good and exceedingly playful,
And to the Kanines he was very grateful.
But this big black dog, black as a cinder.
Could escape the house before you wink,
Through open door, hatchway, slider or winder.
You would not have time to even think,
Of Bear, the Black Lab Retriever

Dan, while going to work one day,
Espied Bear romping free at play.
He took a hold on big Bear's collar.
"Get back in the house and you behave,
Be a good dog, don't make me holler."
He entered the house like a strange cave,
Bear, the Black Lab Retriever.

Olive was about to close the door,
When out on the lawn of the people next door
Was Bear lying on his back sunning.
She puckered her lips and gave a whistle.
Bear jumped up and came a running.
Into the house he shot like a missile.
Bear, the Black Lab Retriever.

George was waiting with friends for the bus.
When suddenly he began to fuss.
For there was Bear sitting by a tree,
Wagging his tail and seeking attention.
"How does this dog find a way to get free?"
George took him home and gave him detention.
Bear, the Black Lab Retriever.

Susan left last chewing on a crust,
But there was Bear rolling in the dust.
"You naughty dog. How is it you're able,
To escape the house without a trace,
Faster than I can get from the table?'
She pushed and pulled and got him in place.
Bear, the Black Lab Retriever.

And then as rare as bright sunny weather,
The Kanines came home at once altogether.
Inside the house to their surprise,
Were three black dogs and a little black bear,
All of them just about the same size.
And out on the lawn, innocent there,
was Bear, the Black Lab Retriever

There's a moral to this story.
Please listen lads and lasses.
When you go out to hunt for Bear,

be sure to wear your glasses.
For if you don't, when you return,
It isn't Bear that you'll discern
For the only one not waiting there
Is Bear, the Black Lab Retriever.

This poem is dedicated to the wonderful children of Hebron Village
School and to their devoted teachers. June 7, 1998

Baker Canoe Trip

We promised the youngsters to take them canoeing
A nice recess from Christian Ed pursuing.
We scouted the Baker, checked the depth of the water.
There was barely enough in this calendar quarter.

From bridge to rest stop the miles where eight.
With any luck the weather'd be great.
A spectacular view would be ours all the way
As we paddled along on Columbus Day.

Our plans were faultless, the weather broke clear,
Cold, slow and shallow did the Baker appear.
We lowered the canoes gently over the rocks.
We didn't know John would soon lose his socks.

John and Nathan's canoe had a fight with a tree
As they entered the water with a loud, WOOEE!
John's jacket went one way, his socks went another
They remain in the water for someone else to discover.

Doug and Lee did great except for a limb.
That's when they too decided to swim.
They liked it so much the first time they dumped
A short time later in the Baker they jumped.

Voss and Zack in the canoe, the ultimate winners,
Were the first to arrive and partake of their dinners.
They were followed by Andy with Jason a raving
On board was Lee, whom they oft had been saving.

There's a moral to our story you all should know
Leave dry clothes at the rest stop before you go.
Eight miles by road is twenty by sea.
And the next time you go don't invite me.

Another Penny for Your Thoughts

It seems to me the Post Office has lost all its sense.
It keeps on asking you and me to surrender sense and cents.

While Publishers Clearing House and Reader's Digest fill our postal
sacks.
And our poor carriers lift and carry their loads upon their backs.

This nuisance mail arrives each day and pains me alack, alas.
Charge them two cents and leave me alone. Or is that too crass?

But, then again, why should I complain about the cost of a letter?
For if I listen to politicians, why--I never had it better.

I dispose of all my entries, and give up all my chances,
And fill my garbage bag with them, and risk my trash man's glances.

Save a tree!
Charge them, not me!

Sweeter Than All the Rest

This toddling child with pretty frock,
Came across the field so grand.
Her soiled gloves a mother's shock,
Yellow dandelions in hand.
She held them out with a beautiful smile.
Said, "I love Mimi," which means mother.
And she knew at once, not in a while,
She loved her like no other.

The boy arrived with corsage in hand,
An orchid sweet, pretty, and yellow.
He tied it on with ribbon band,
The nervous, tongue-tied young fellow.
How lovely and loved she has become.
She's sweet sixteen and now dating.
Mom paces anxiously at home,
While for her sweet child she's waiting.

It came with a card, in a box rectangular,
One yellow rose just meant for her.
From this quiet young man so angular.
But, to her eyes it brought a tear.
Mom and Pop shared cautious glances.
For they remember when Dad had sent,
The same to test his chances.
A little spot in their heart was rent.

She came with red rose and wearing a ring.
The young man was pale and awkward.
But he had the strength to ask the thing,
That we all know would soon be offered.
The wedding bouquet was of daises, sweet,
And the bride and groom were handsome.

They left together the world to greet,
And as one, crossed another transom.

He stood beside her alert and proud,
For they were now mother and father.
New parents floating on a cloud,
This boy would be no bother.
He presented her with daffodils sweet,
While the world seemed sort of blurry.
From a vendor on the street,
He had bought them in a hurry.

The little boy balanced on legs just learning,
Wallowing eager in sweet spring field.
His mother sat, heart within her turning.
He plucked flowering, golden yield.
He came stumbling back in his little fist tight,
Dandelions brought memories of her mother.
When she was a child and love was in flight.
"This is the best bouquet son, like none other."

She's older now with dear granddaughter.
Who calls her Nana, (just dainty as nails).
But she picks dandelions, nobody taught her,
Just for Grandma in colorful pails.
No matter how old our heroine gets,
She sees love in this simplest of flowers.
And looks back at life with no regrets.
How they brightened her grandest of hours.

Great Grandma lies still on her bier,
And flowers, all colors, surround her.
And love ones pause for hidden back there
Where they will cause no one bother.
See, in the back you can spy them.

Are dandelions great grandson has brought
For no one could think to deny him.
His great love, for great grandma, no doubt!

Her spirit resides in heaven in peace,
Her body is here in the graveyard.
Little children come by and blow the fleece.
The seeds that sail billowy skyward.
And forever assure that this gardener's pest,
This flower you present like none other.
Will always be sweeter than all the rest,
When given by child to a mother.

Sarah

Translucent Memories

Chasing after the child on the tricycle
Who rides ahead of me in a dream
 Her silver laughter filling the air
I find myself on the beach and see her
Pretending to control the water
By casting it into the sky like fairy dust
Blue melds into blue, where one is false, only a reflection
The sandals I wear on my rough, sand kissed feet
Have battle scars
Rips from chasing so frantically after that child
Who runs towards a future only I
And the angels have an inkling of
I try to raise my hoarse voice to tell her to stop
Or she'll become like the water, reflective of her
surroundings
Her true colors masked

Missing Wings

There is a little girl
Her small hands playing God
Molding the sand into a castle
The place where she dreams
A beautiful princess and her prince dwell
I watch from the water, smiling
Then sulk with her as the castle falls
To the mighty water dragon
I wonder what her future will be
Contemplate what I thought at that age
I wanted to fly with the birds
The lonely mourning dove I heard every morning
Tell it not to cry anymore
My wings have yet to grow
I'm starting to think I don't have any

Dian West

Driving 6:45 A.M.

In the early morning
on the still pond
the sun glistens on
the "V" shaped wake
that follows
the lone duck
swimming in search
of his morning meal.

For Davina 05/6/12

A small soft
fuzzy head
snuggles against
Grammy's neck
all sweetness
embodied in
one precious little girl.

For Lin

I hurt my friend
my friend, who I love dearly,
by holding our friendship
deep in my heart.
Not letting it breathe
and grow and blossom.
Not tending to our friendship
with kindness and care.
For this I am truly sorry.

First Night

Hot and sultry
The air
Fills the senses
With the promise
Of summer nights to come

Forest Lights

In the twilight
the gentle wind
rustles the leaves
in the hard woods
behind the pines.
Causing the illusion
of twinkle lights
in the forest.

Missing Mom Meese

I reach for phone
then I remember.
I go about my chores
as if nothing has changed
then a wave rolls over
bringing the tears.
I reach for the phone
then I remember
she isn't there.

Carol White

November Day

Judging by the numbers of cars left by the roadsides, the hunters are out in force. I can't blame them. I don't hunt, but there is a powerful pull to get out and walk the woods before winter closes down. On a classic late November morning, brilliantly sunny, breathlessly still, and penetratingly chill, I like to take my dog walking along a trail cut through our woods. Frost glazed beech leaves crunch underfoot and deep shadows underlay the evergreens; black in contrast to the bright sunshine. Along the many rills and streams running down the hillsides there is a light rime of ice where water splashed and froze overnight. It's a different, more austere beauty than the fresh greens of spring or the brilliance of the early fall. Everything seems clearer, in closer focus. The earth smells sharply of moisture and old leaves.

I wear a blaze orange hat and vest with reflective stripes. My dog, a large sable German Shepherd, could possibly, if one is half blind and none too careful, resemble a deer. Therefore we have matching blaze orange ensembles and we both wear cowbells. Who could miss us? So far everybody has. Missed us that is.

Yes, it did happen. The one idiot that did shoot at us did miss. At that time I was accompanied by not one, but a pair of brilliantly garbed Shepherds. As we came clanging through our back woods, heading towards a power line cut, I heard a shotgun discharge and pellets rained down around us. When I screeched in shock and ire, heading for the ground, a second shot followed. I then bellowed that he was on private property and had 10 seconds to clear out. A head to toe camouflaged figure popped up from the brush and started running. To urge him on I yelled to the dogs, "Get him boys." The dogs had no idea what the words meant, but if he would run they would play too, and romped after him. He improved on his head start considerably. One whistle called the reluctant dogs back. The shooter jumped in his car, leaving a rooster tail of gravel as he chewed his way back to the power lines. We were all of us lucky that day.

In the years since then our walks have been less exciting. The few hunters I've met in the woods have been courteous especially when you consider that we've possibly scared off every wild animal for acres around. Or maybe not. We've flushed a few turkeys and grouse along our way. No deer though. I only see them in my garden. Our walks continue, perhaps adding a scarf and mittens, until that day when white flakes fill the air. Looking up makes them stick in my eyelashes and make tiny chill spots on my cheeks. From then on I leave the trails for those more athletic types who snowshoe and cross country ski the back trails, and the roving packs of snowmobilers. No, I don't mind them a bit. They save me a good bit of hard work clearing trails. It's only fair that they get the winter trails since I enjoy them the rest of the year.

Fishing Day

Newfound Lake, despite really low temperatures was refusing to freeze. Howling northwest gales churned the surface into whitecaps not allowing the lake to freeze over. At the southern tip of the lake, sheets and panes of transparent ice, thinner than window glass, were being piled up on the shore. Delicate pieces would form and be blown to the south bay.

First there was a thin rim around the bay, like the salt on a margarita, but as the days went by the ice rim grew and extended until I could not tell where the land stopped and the water started. Then it crept up the sides of the lake and out into the bay, 10 feet, 30 feet, 50 feet. When the wind finally calmed the bay froze in a gleaming, slick surface so clear the dark waters beneath appeared like black marble. The deepest waters remained open.

So when I drove by the very recently iced over lake on a Friday morning not too long ago, I did a double take. Sure enough there was an ice fishing shack out there, maybe a hundred feet from shore and about halfway between that shore and the still open water. Who went and put it out there? Probably a direct descendent of the first guy to eat an oyster. Some people will try anything.

Nevertheless I have to admit that I enjoy watching the ice fishing villages go up. It brings life and color to the monochrome of white snow and ice. By Monday, if the ice is thick enough, there will be several clusters of bobhouses with people zipping between them on snowmobiles. There are migrations of "sleds" across the frozen lake like mechanical mastodons, huge and noisy with their "mahouts" swathed in polar fleece and suits like astronauts. They travel in clusters, families, and clubs. If you see one sled screaming across the ice, you can be pretty sure he is traveling between groups, perhaps a courier delivering some urgent package, like a six pack to parched denizens of a fishing shack. I don't really KNOW what's going on out there, but I have a good deal of fun imagining it. I suspect that for generations it has been mostly a way for guys to get out of the house away from the wife and kids during the winter. That doesn't necessarily hold true anymore.

Once the ice fishing enclaves are set up, a whole winter culture evolves. Coolers are ferried out to the shacks, grills are set up on the ice, friends visit back and forth across the lake, and kids roll around on the ice like seal pups. As I drive by the shore on a cold, sunny day I can smell hamburgers grilling. When I drop in at the Newfound Grocery or the Small Mart they have extra clerks working to provide the ice fishermen and their families with the necessities of polar existence. A splendid example of interdependence: social bonding and building the local economy all at the same time.

Other than being small and temporary there is little similarity among the bobhouses. They range from a propane heated, slide- in camper removed from its truck, to a brilliant yellow house of four glued together panels of solid foam (insulation?) secured to heavy wooden runners. Some are painted with cartoon characters or flowers. Others are made of old scrap wood planks. Some look to be transplanted garden sheds. Then there are those people who simply drill a hole in the ice and drop a line through. No shack. No grill. Just a hole in the ice. Brrr. I am assuming they are the purists of the ice fishing world.

I wonder what determines the shacks' placement. Do folks encamp together as friends or because they think the fishing is good there? Or because everyone thinks the first guy probably knows what he's doing and the rest follow suit? One day I will knock on a few doors and ask.

So, in spite of the fact that I look with trepidation on those first few icehouses, and I do harbor a few small doubts about the sanity of anyone who would go out and fish on the ice, with or without a fishing shack, I love seeing the fishing tribes arrive on the lakes each winter. Welcome back.

Fog Sprites Day

We live "between." Our home is tucked between the Lakes and the White Mountains, close to a large lake, but perched on the knees of the mountains. We aren't at lake level, but we aren't so very high up either. This location means we get what I can only call "between weather". It's half past winter, but not yet spring or autumn is past, the trees have lost their leaves, but there's no snow yet. It's between type weather. It's chill, it's damp, and mostly it's fog. When the temperatures at night are in the twenties, but days are (barely) above freezing we have fog in the evenings and mornings. Freezing, icy fog.

This morning the lake was entirely still, but so shrouded in fog that it was simply a bowl of clouds. The mist wafted in twisting columns upwards and away from the lake, each column branching and reaching upwards. It's easy to see sprites dancing on the lakes surface. As the fog glides from the lake it touches everything from twigs at the tops of the pines to leaves by the roadside with a thick rime of sparkling frost. The fog swirls around the highest branches of the trees and coasts along the tops of the hills, hiding everything, drawing aside to reveal glimpses of glittering fairylands. (And watch the steps on your way down the walk.) The sun becomes a bright spot in the sky, a silver dime. As it breaks through the low banks of cloud, the world floods with brilliance. It is spectacular. Almost blinding light shatters and is thrown back from every surface. Rainbows spark across the hillsides. For a few breaths the world is transformed into a crystalline work of art. As with all things of surpassing beauty, it is transient. The sunlight that fires the brilliance also destroys it, melting it in moments. The light frost on the trees effervesces into the air leaving mundane twigs and bark in place of crystal. Once the fog lifts completely, the lake is as calm as a millpond. The sprites have ceased their dance. Every hill and tree is reflected in the water's surface, a perfect mirror waiting to reflect the next season.

Meteor Showers

Nights are for sleeping. That is my usual motto, but there are times when I forsake my diurnal nature and await with great anticipation the progress of the night. The big question on those nights is, will the sky stay clear? These are the nights when the various meteor showers are forecast. What could be better than hours of fireworks? I love to observe these, nature's own fireworks, the meteor showers. A favorite are the Geminids. They have rarely disappointed me. December in New Hampshire is not known for clear skies. It can be foggy, rainy or snow in feet instead of inches, but when it is clear, I dress for the Arctic and sit out there watching. There's not much point in going out before 2 or 3 am, but I have my long down coat with my favorite gloves at the ready and a folding chair to put on the front lawn. Since the coldest nights seem to be the clearest it pays to be ready to bundle up. Sometimes the meteors have been amazing, but the deep night, normally so unfamiliar to me, is lovely in its own right. I enjoy seeing the bare trees with brilliant stars like strands of diamonds caught up among their bare branches. With the air so still and sharp, the woods black and as still as the sky, it is a completely different world than the daytime one.

I try not to anticipate the meteors too much. The best approach seems to be to consider it a win/win situation. If I wake up and the sky is clear I can watch the Geminids. If the sky is clouded over I'll go back to bed and possibly make it through the next day without falling asleep by 4pm. My better half said he'd be willing to watch if they would just hold the showers " at a reasonable time of day."

This year I was lucky. I got up just before 3am, donned all of my wool and down, microwaved a cup of tea, and went out to watch the meteor shower. It was great. I have a rather small area of clear sky, not much more than directly overhead, but I did still see a lot of beautiful shooting stars. I apologize to technical purists, but it is such a visually appropriate term. There were good sized ones, making brushstrokes of milky light or even sizzling across the sky. There were other little quick sparks and dashes, and what may have been a satellite or possibly an airliner very high. I never know how many an hour I see as time simply slides by.

At about 5 am the edges of the horizon began to grow milky. The tendrils of opacity mounted, reaching into the dome of the black sky. A penetrating chill accompanied the fading of the night sky as the fog grew and swelled to fill all the area from earth to sky. It was time to go back to my warm bed to sleep until daylight, dreaming of celestial visitors and brilliant stars.

Made in the USA
Charleston, SC
28 March 2013